Krampus

Koloring Book

Vol. 2

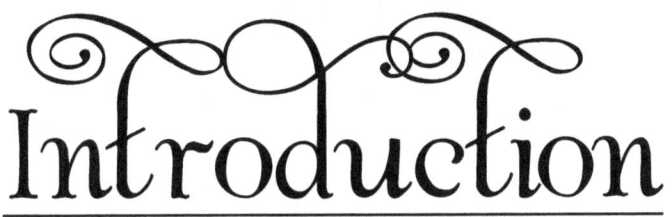

Introduction

THE KRAMPUS. WE MAY HAVE FORGOTTEN THIS DEMONIC COMPANION OF ST. NICKOLAUS FOR A TIME, BUT IT IS CLEAR WE NEED HIM NOW MORE THAN EVER. THE KRAMPUS WOULD ACCOMPANY ST. NICKOLAUS AS THEY JUDGED THE HOPEFUL LITTLE BOYS AND GIRLS AT CHRISTMAS TIME. IF THE CHILDREN WERE GOOD, FROM HIS SACK ST. NICKOLAUS WOULD GIVE THEM GIFTS AND SWEETS. BUT IF THE CHILDREN WERE BAD, ST. NICKOLAUS LEFT THEM TO THE KRAMPUS AND HIS PUNISHMENT.

THE KRAMPUS'S NAME COMES FROM THE OLD NORSE WORD FOR CLAW. THE KRAMPUS IS COVERED IN BLACK FUR, HORNS UPON HIS HEAD WITH CLOVEN HOOVES FOR FEET. HIS TEETH ARE SHARP. THE THORNY SWITCH HE WIELDS STINGS THE SKIN OF NAUGHTY CHILDREN EVERYWHERE. HIS LONG TONGUE THEN LICKS UP THE CHILDREN'S TEARS. IN HIS BASKET, THE KRAMPUS STUFFS THE NAUGHTY CHILDREN TO TAKE THEM TO HIS LAIR, PERHAPS HELL ITSELF. THERE HE WHIPS THEM. THERE HE COOKS THEM. AND THERE HE EATS THEM.

IT'S NO SURPRISE THIS ANCIENT YULETIDE TERROR IS MAKING A COMEBACK. THE MODERN CELEBRATION OF CHRISTMAS DOES ITS' BEST TO MAKE US FORGET HOW AWFUL WE CAN BE. WITH ITS' SHINY AND BRIGHT COMMERCIALISM, THE "GOOD TIDINGS WE BRING" GREETING CARD SCHLOCK, THE HIGH-FRUCTOSE VISIONS OF SUGAR PLUMS DANCING ALONG OUR WAISTLINES, CHRISTMAS TIME HYPNOTIZES US INTO THINKING WE CAN DO NO WRONG, THAT IT'S ALL GOOD. SANTA DOESN'T REALLY CHECK THE NAUGHTY LIST, DOES HE?

BUT THE KRAMPUS KNOWS BETTER. WE HAVE BEEN NAUGHTY LITTLE CHILDREN & THE KRAMPUS IS HERE TO MAKE US PAY!

HAPPY HOLIDAYS, AND HAPPY COLORING!

-     CHRISTIAN J. COLTON
KRAMPUS HISTORIOGRAPHER

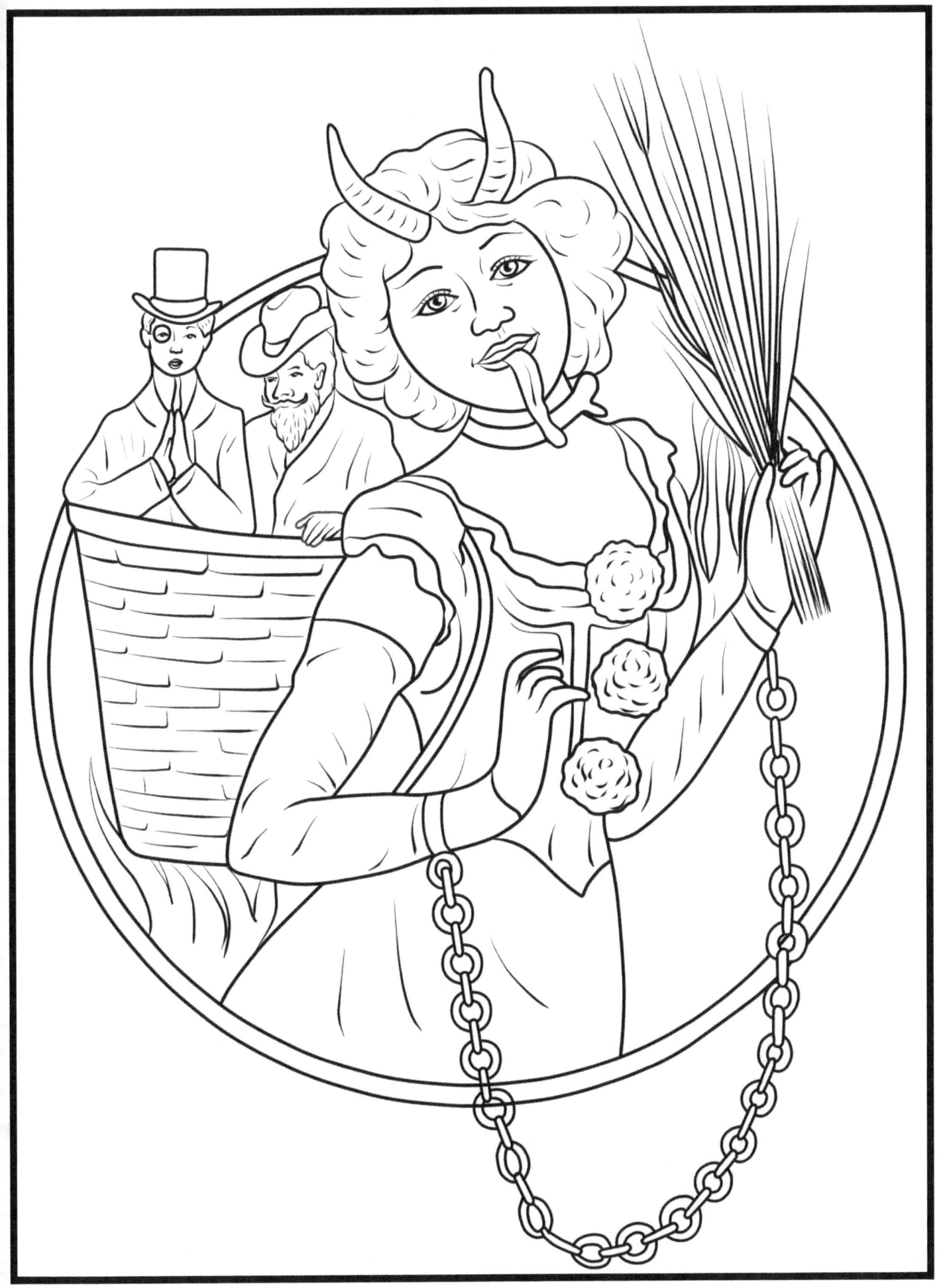

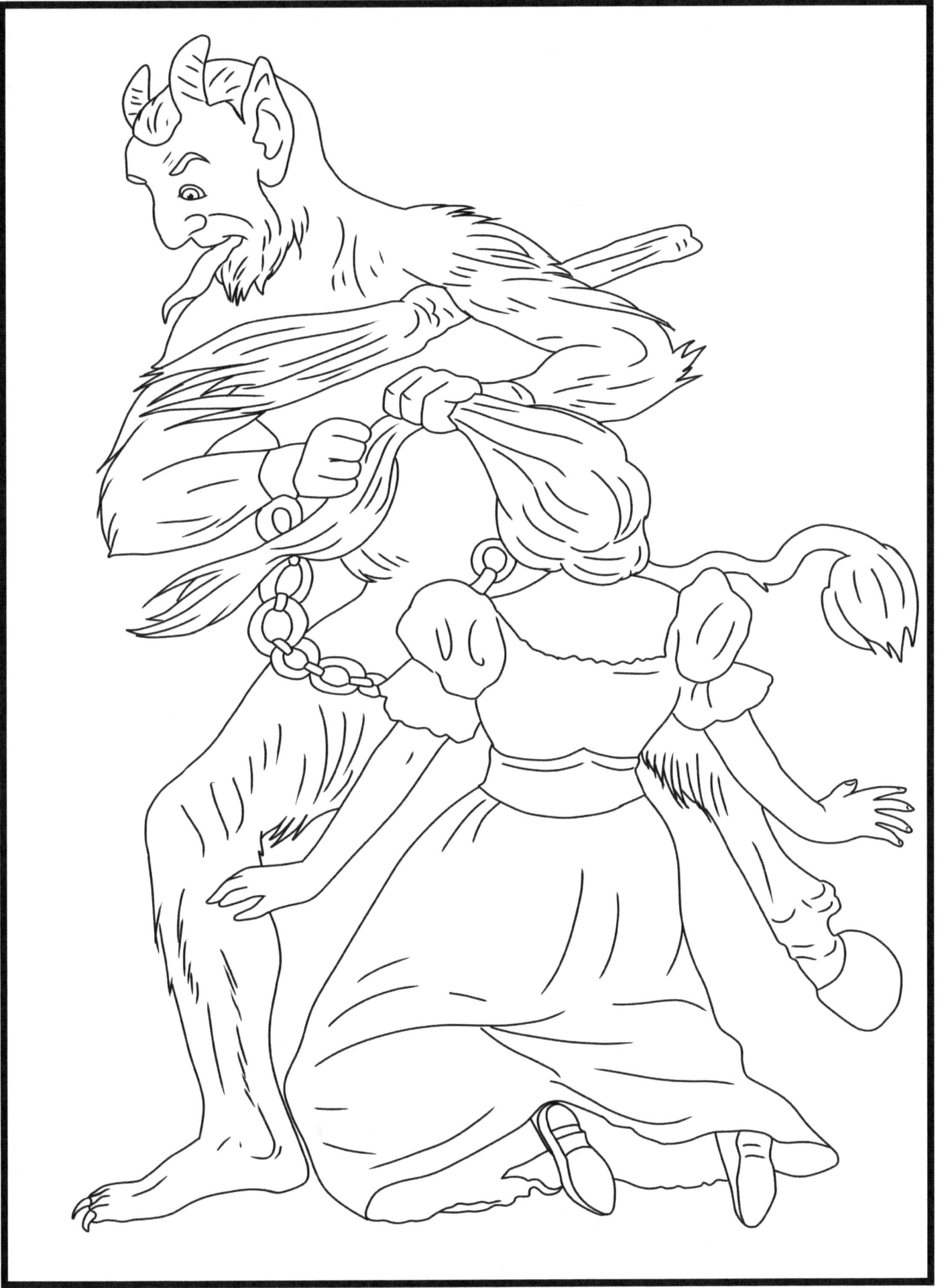

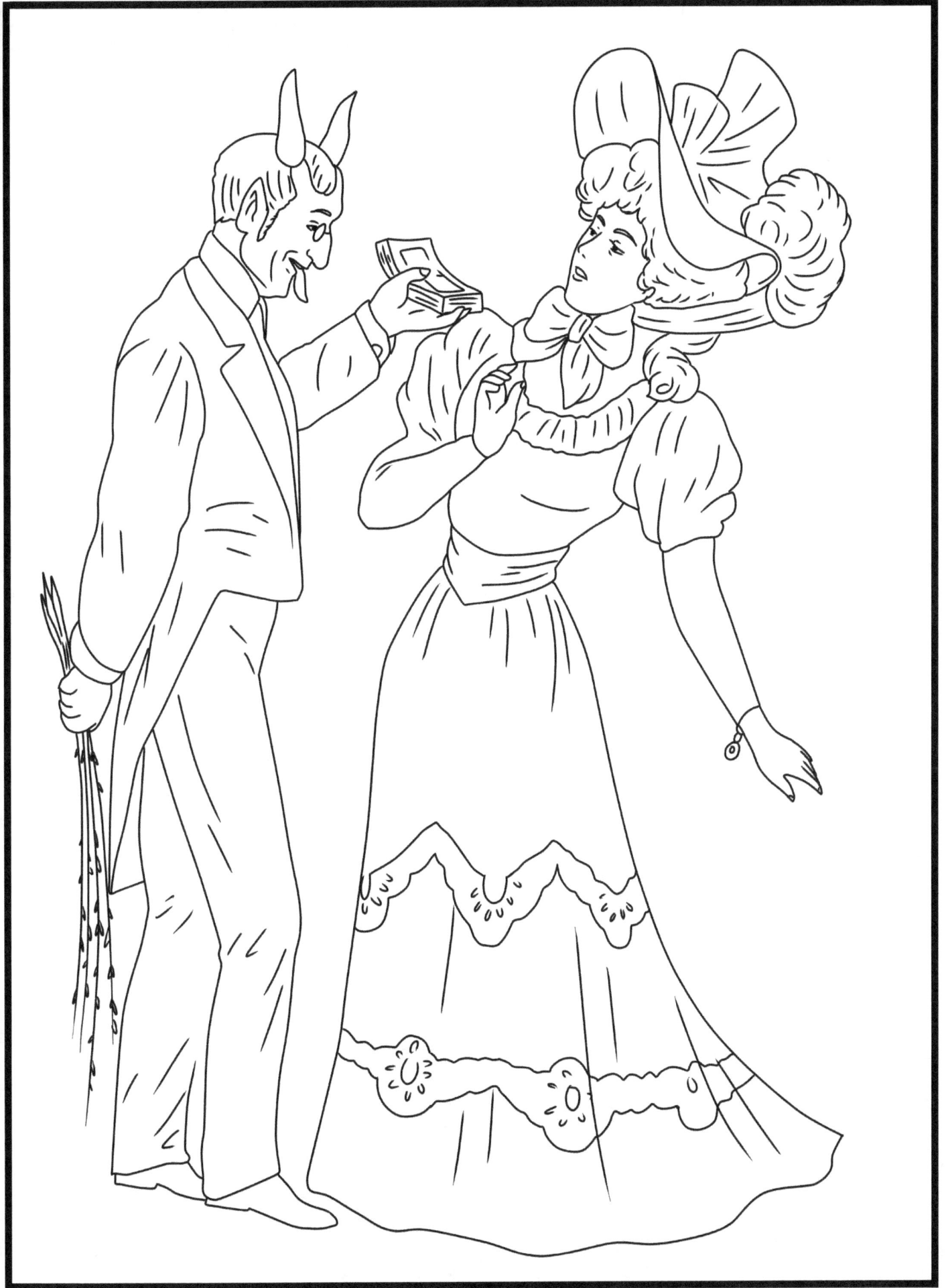

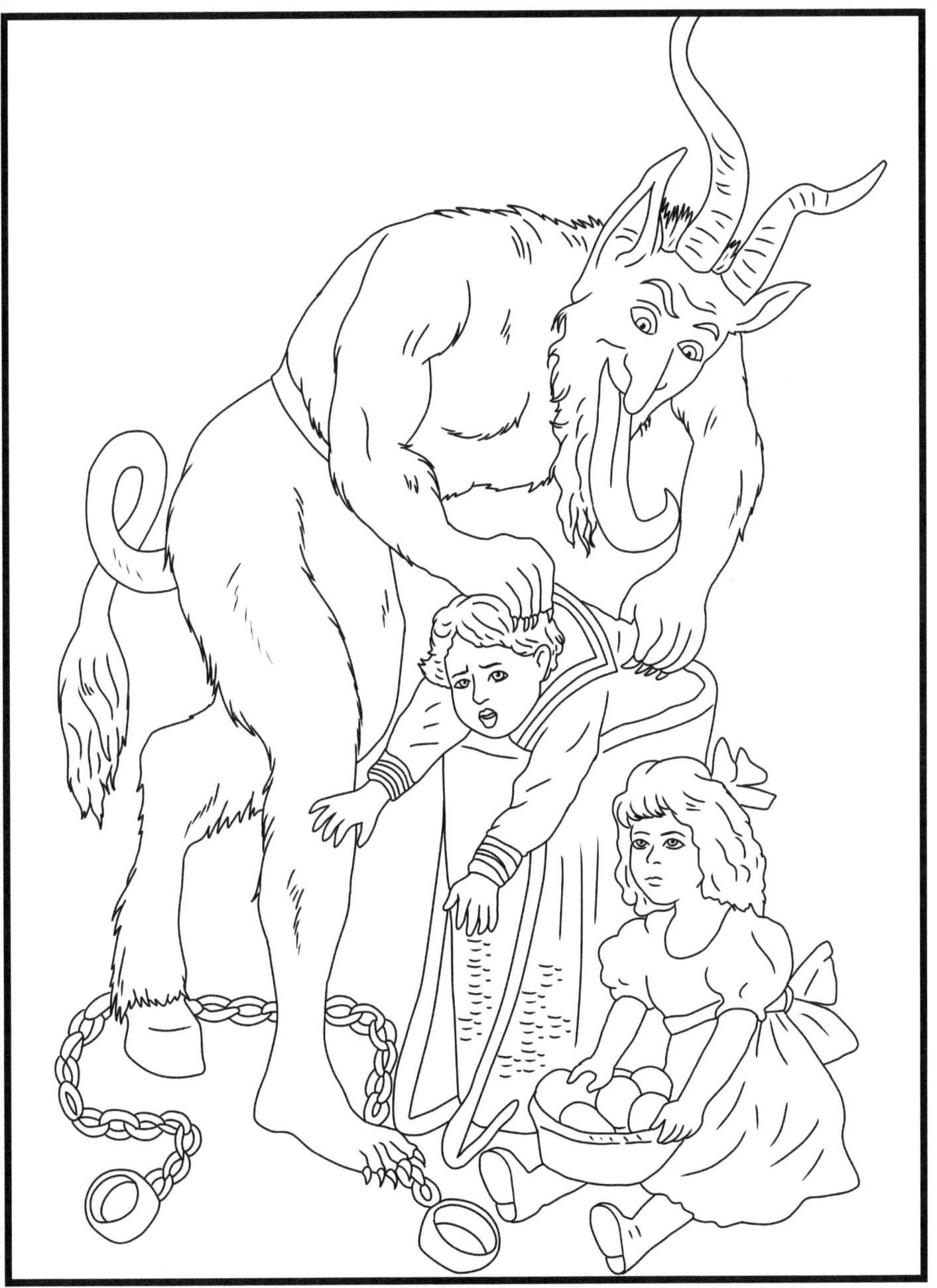

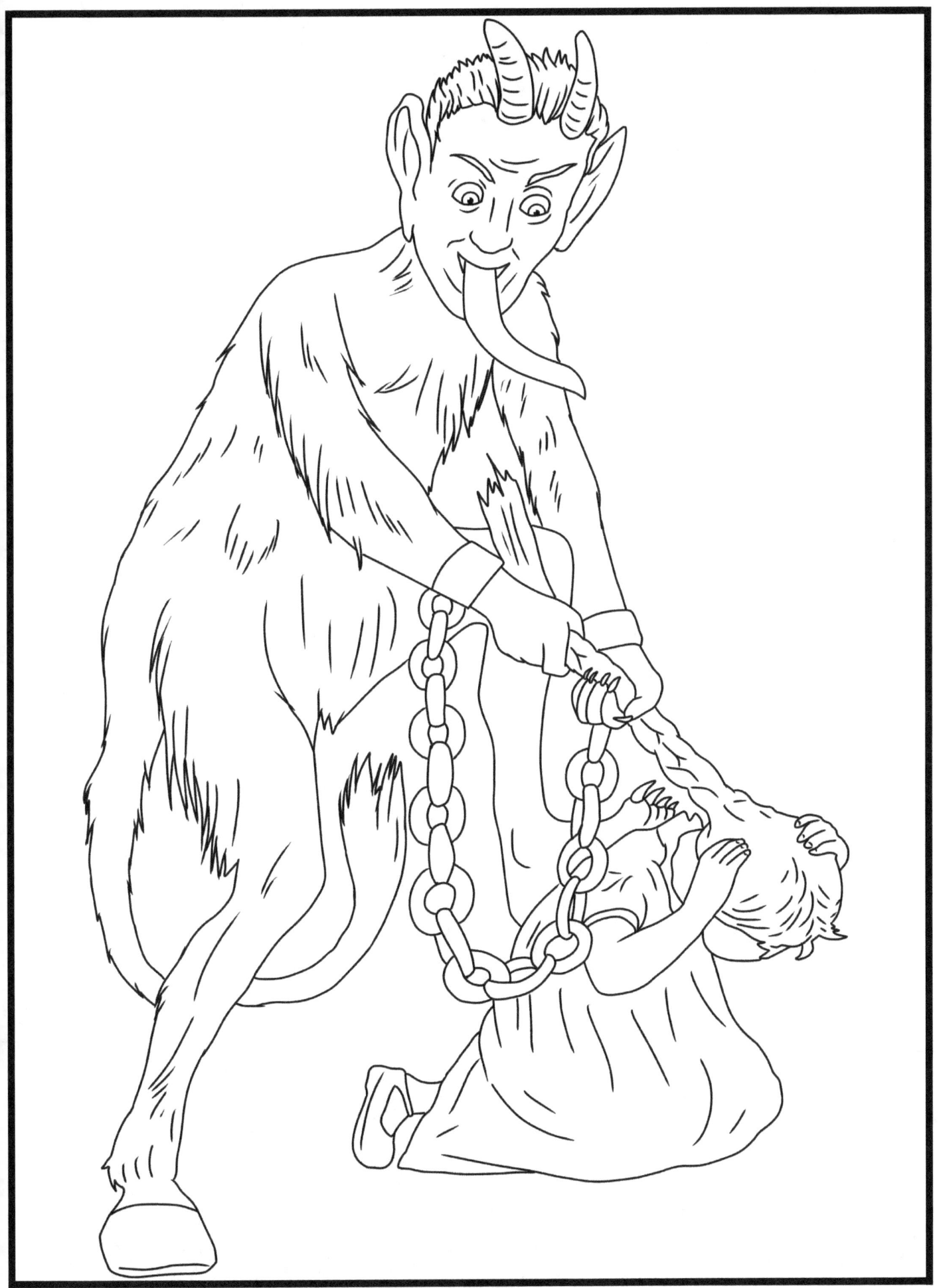

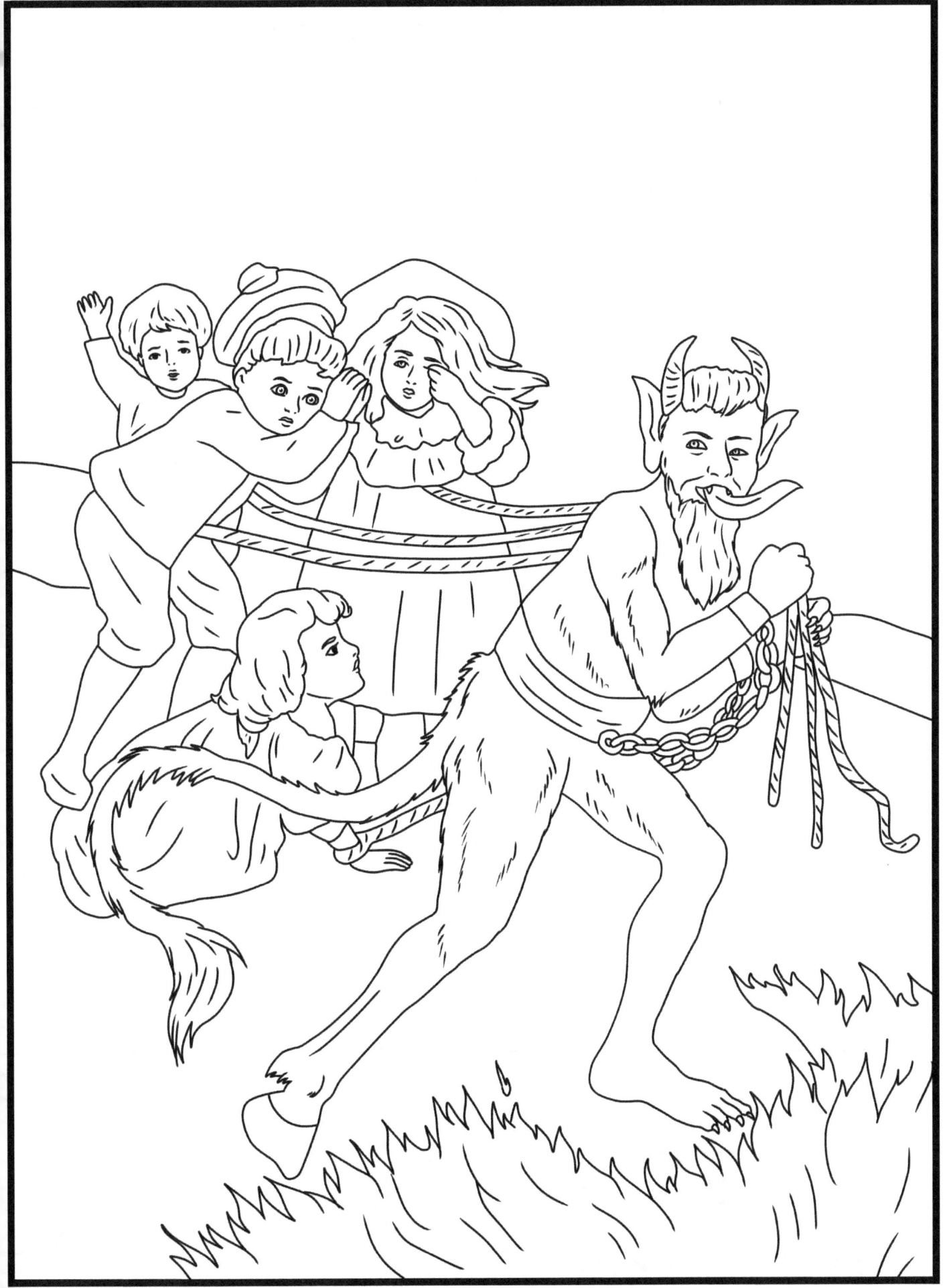

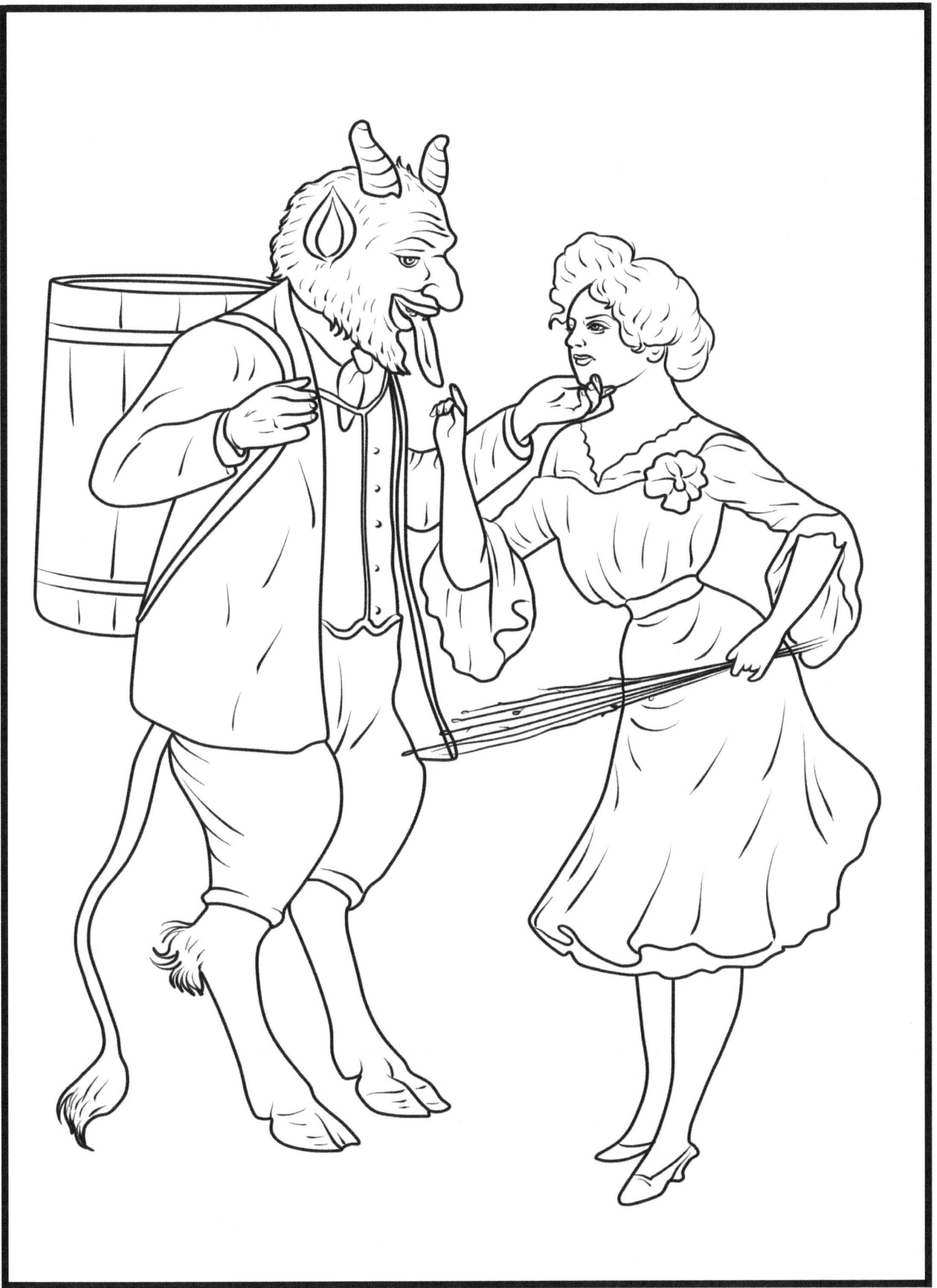

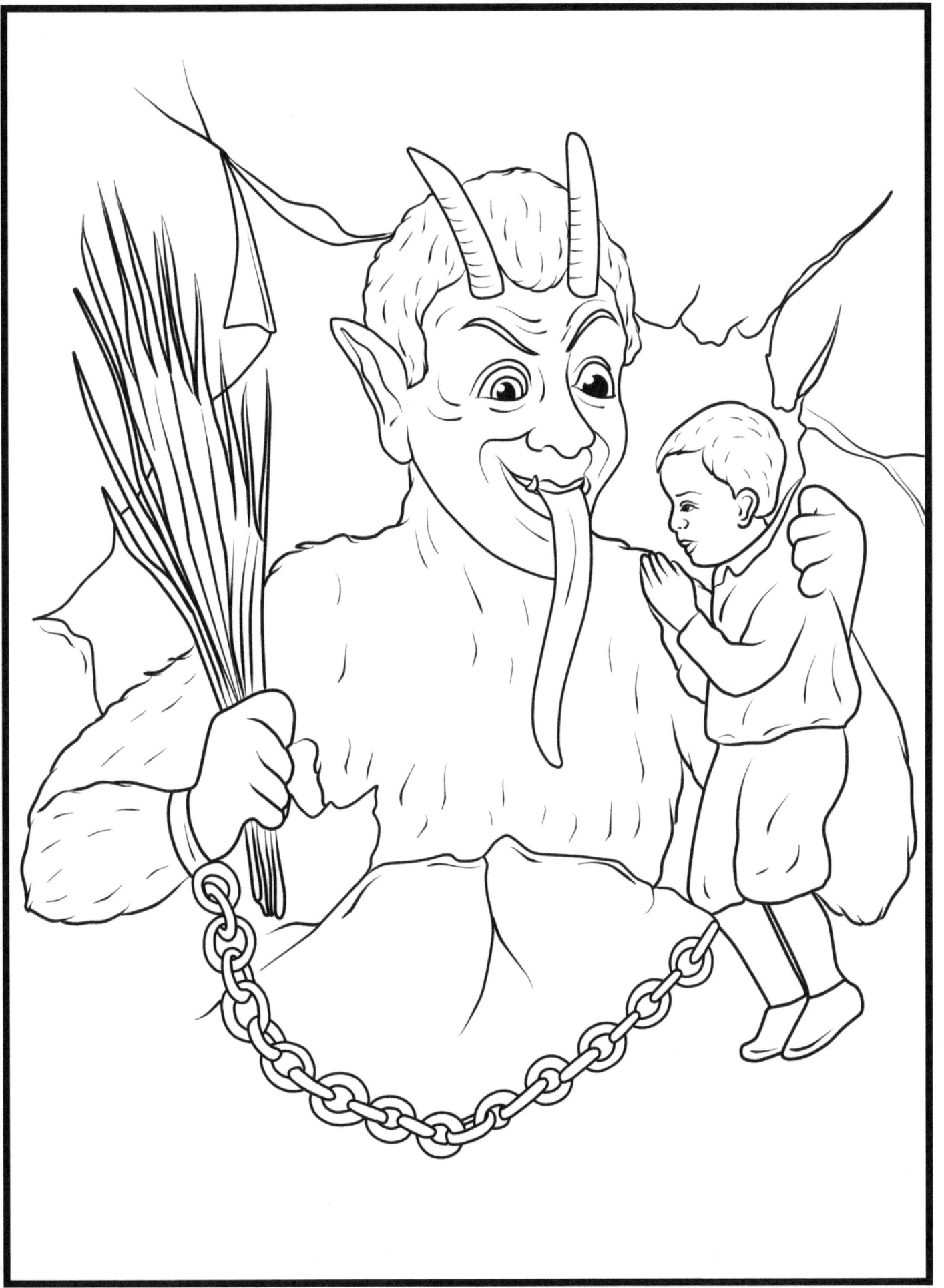

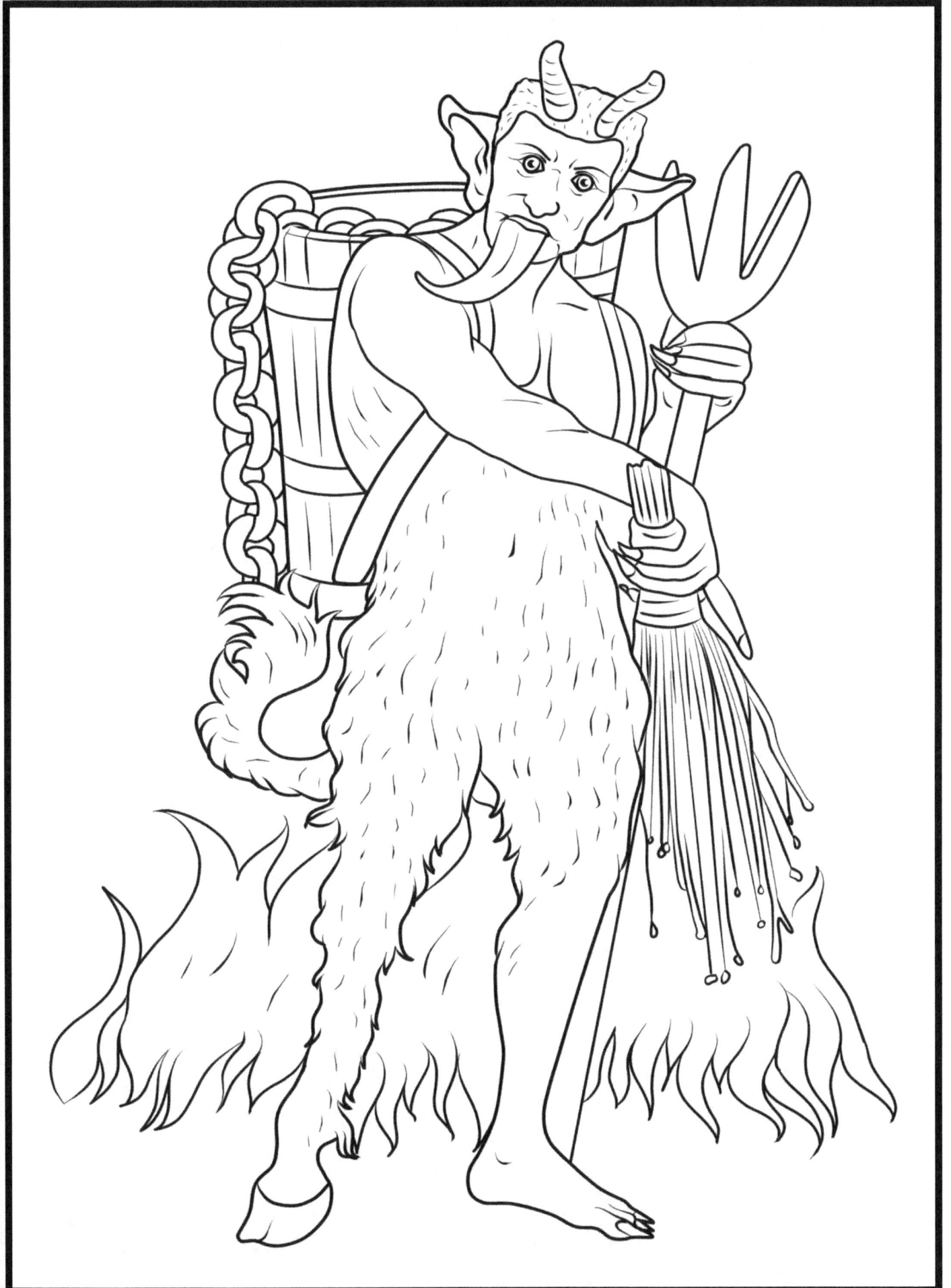

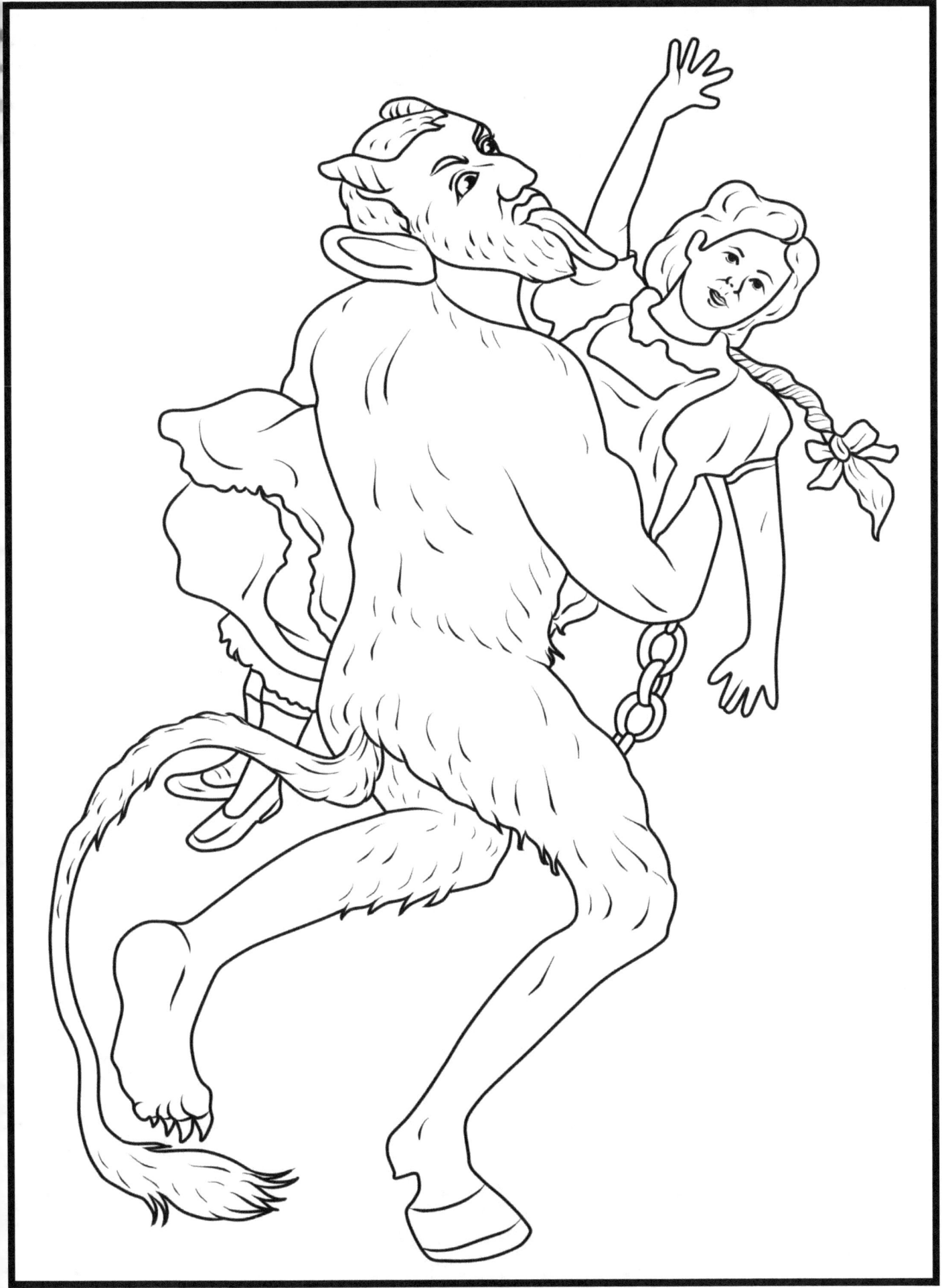

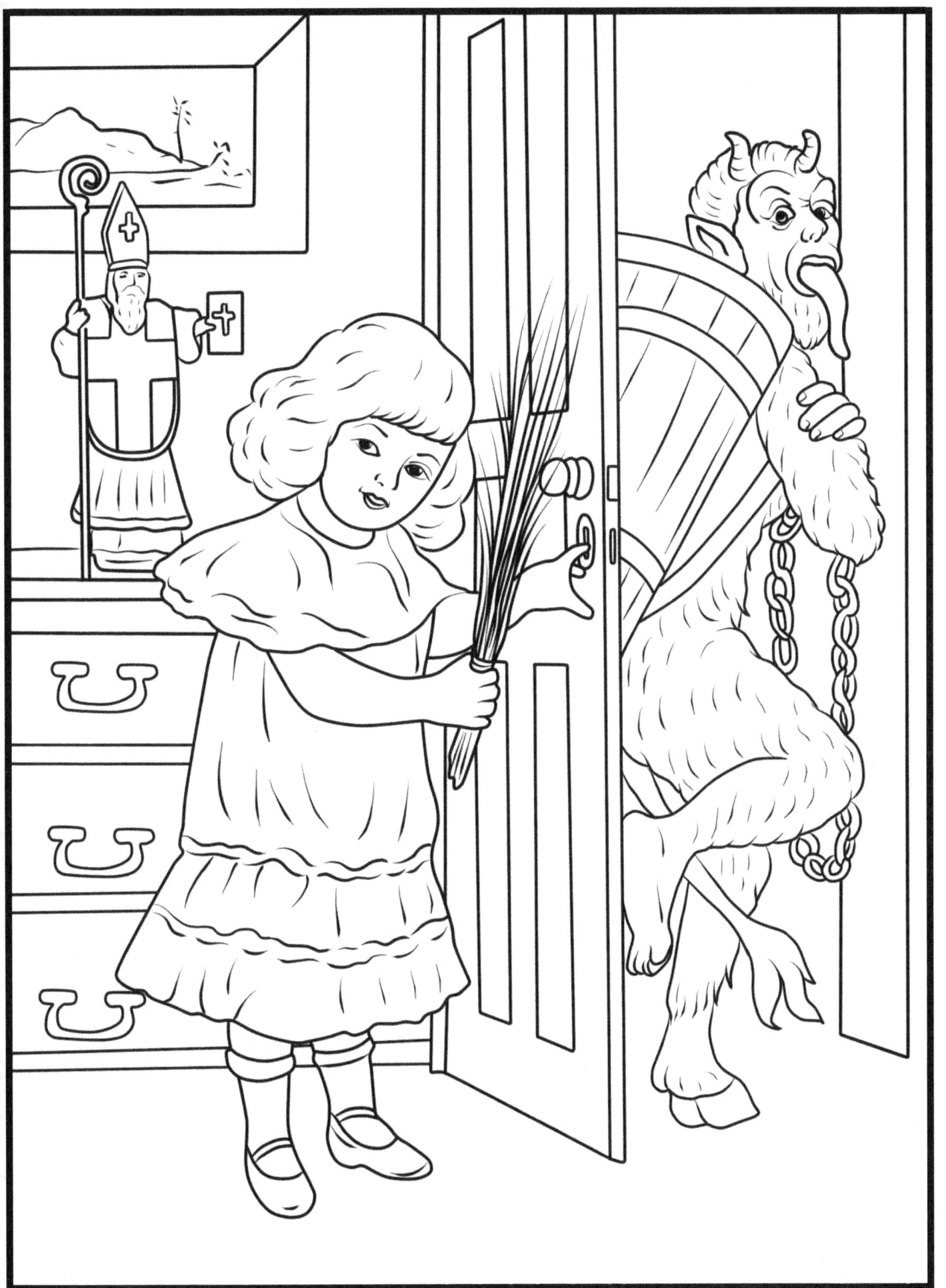

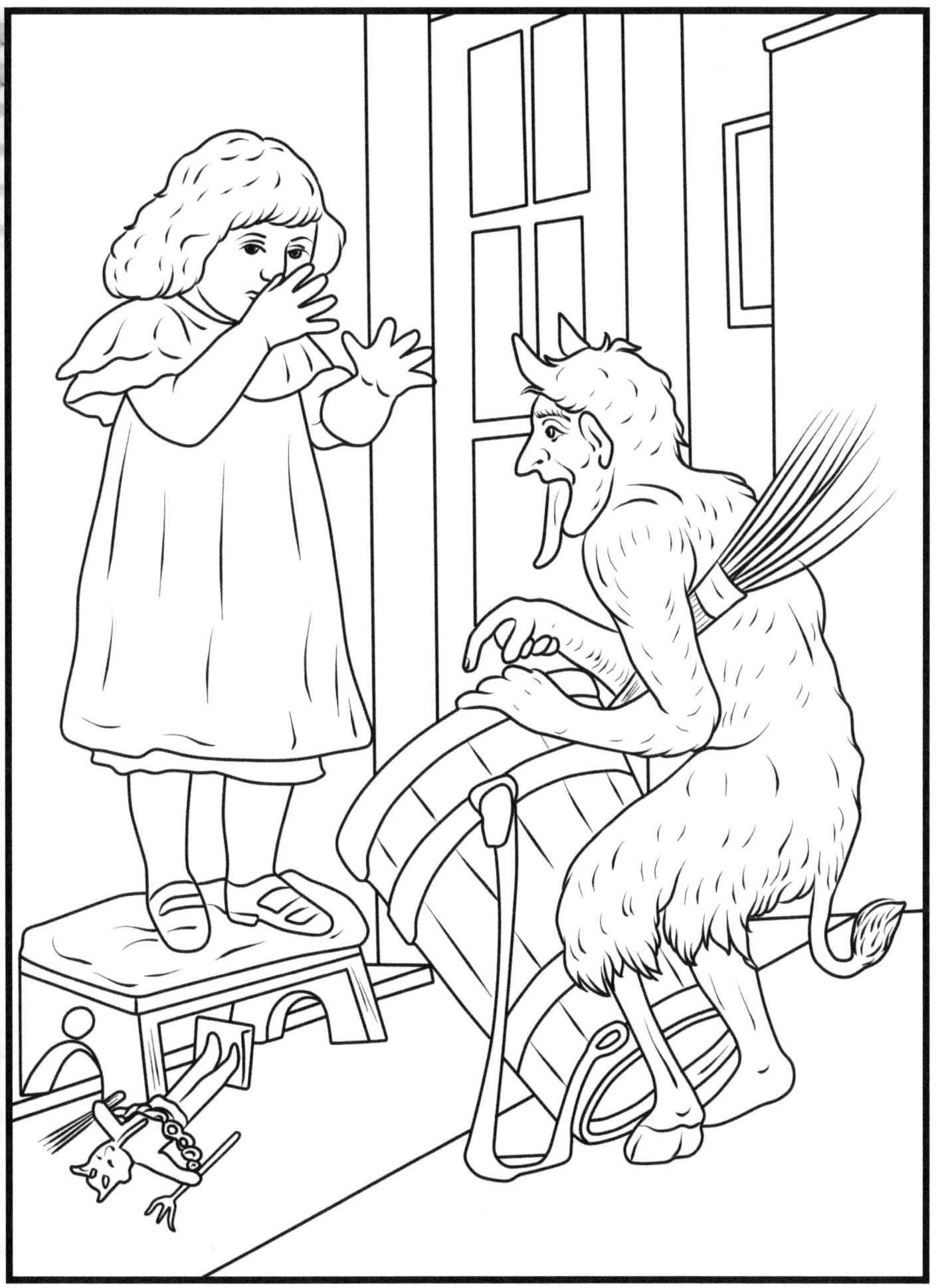

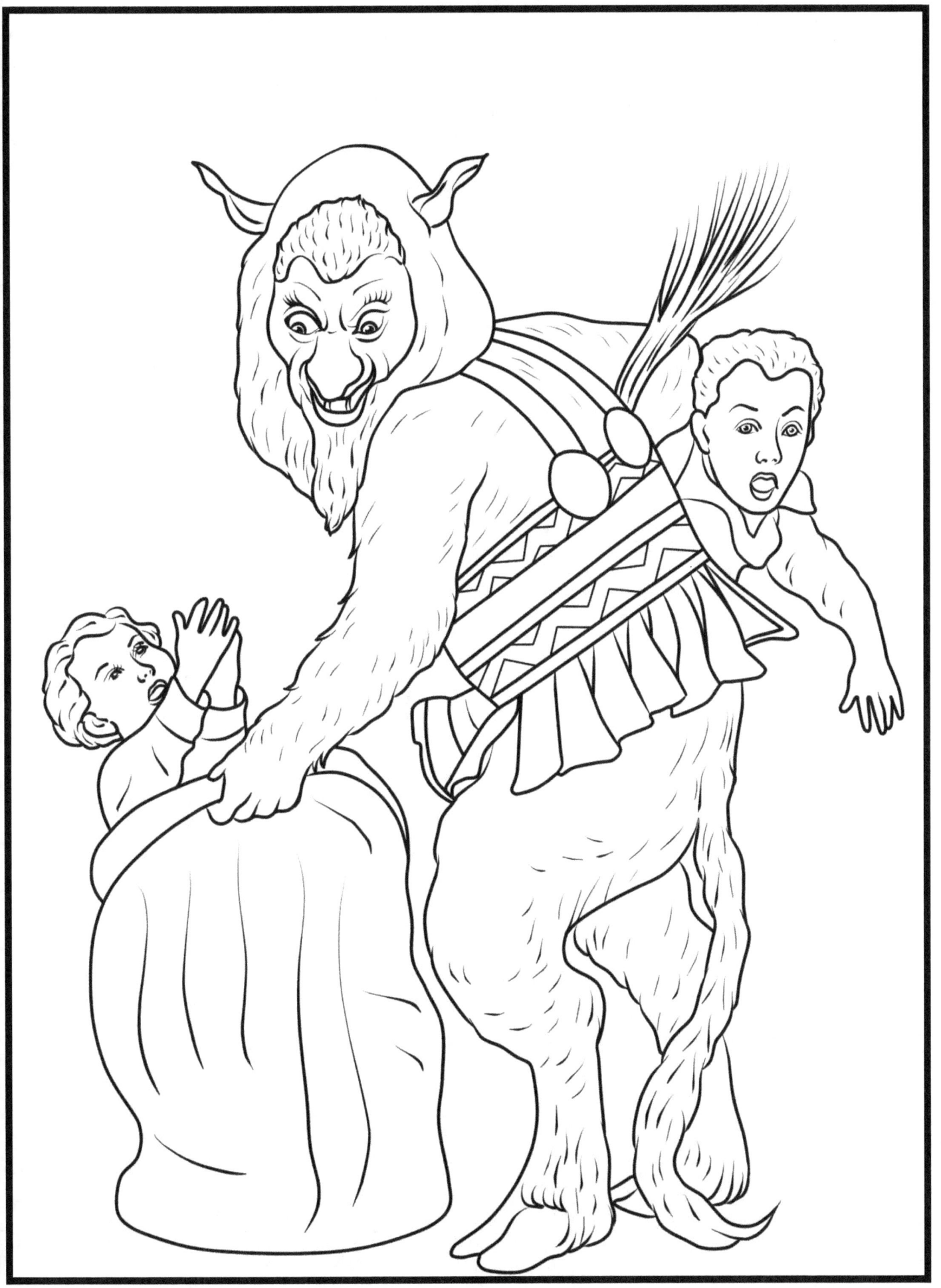

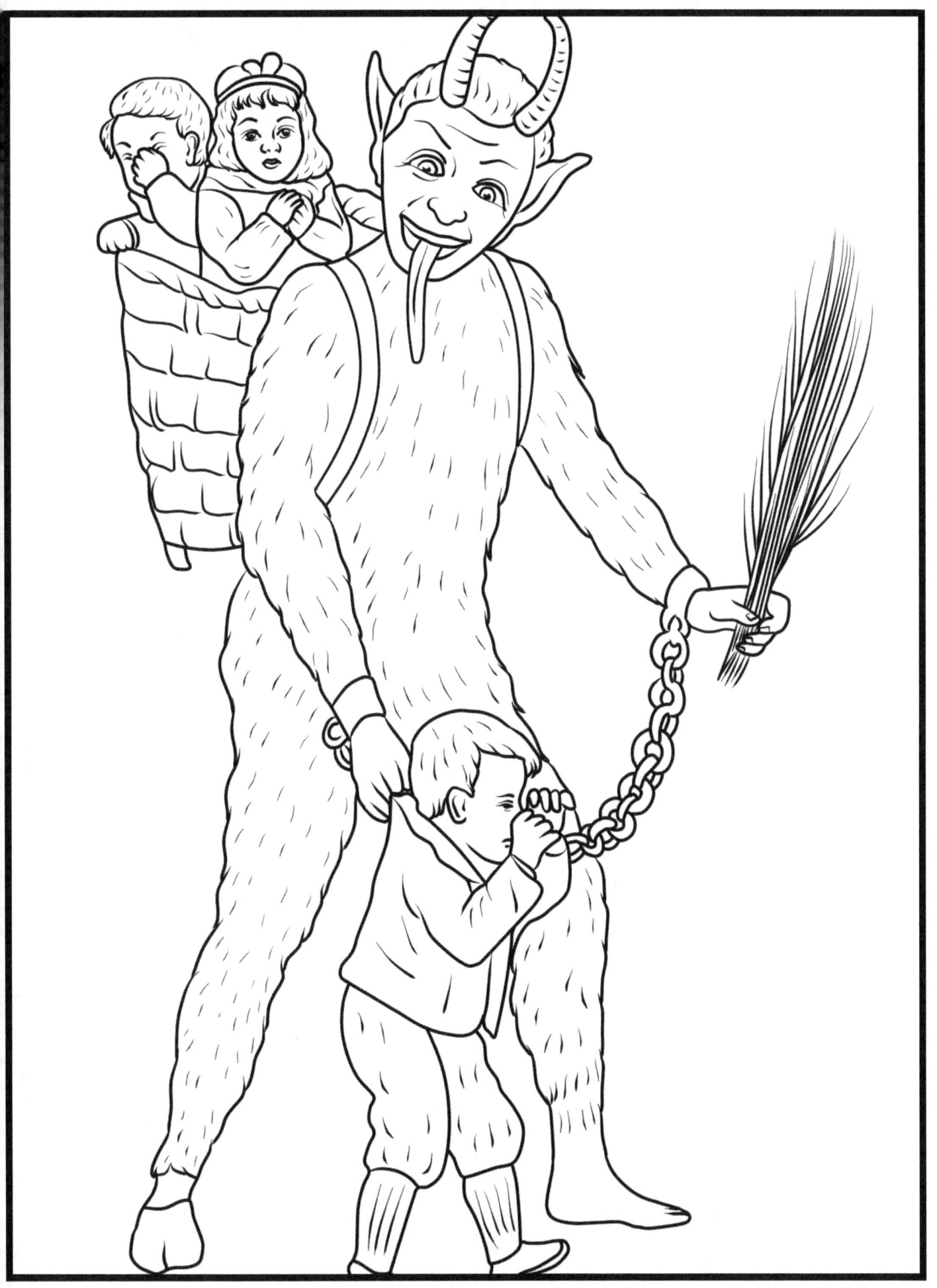

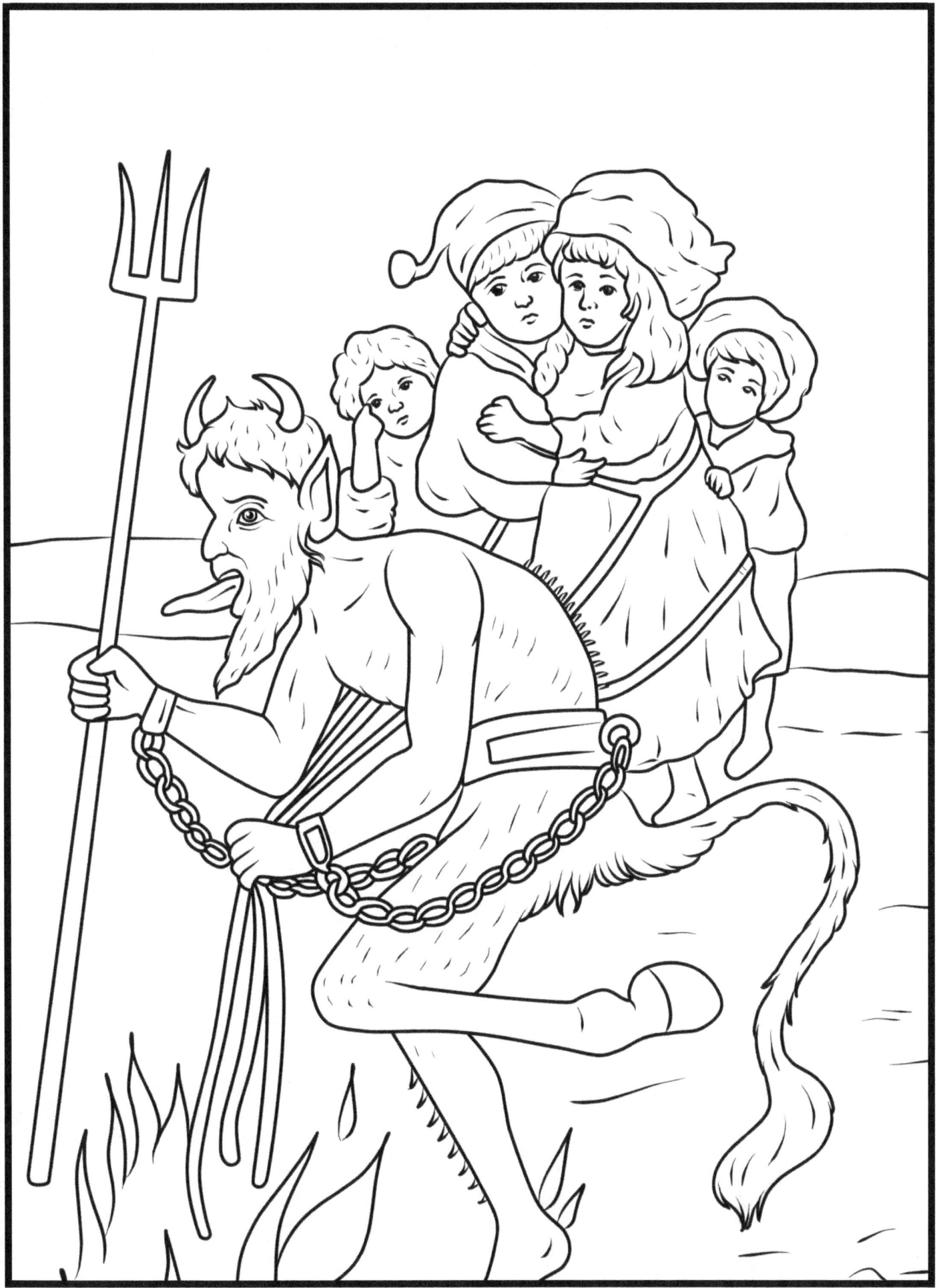

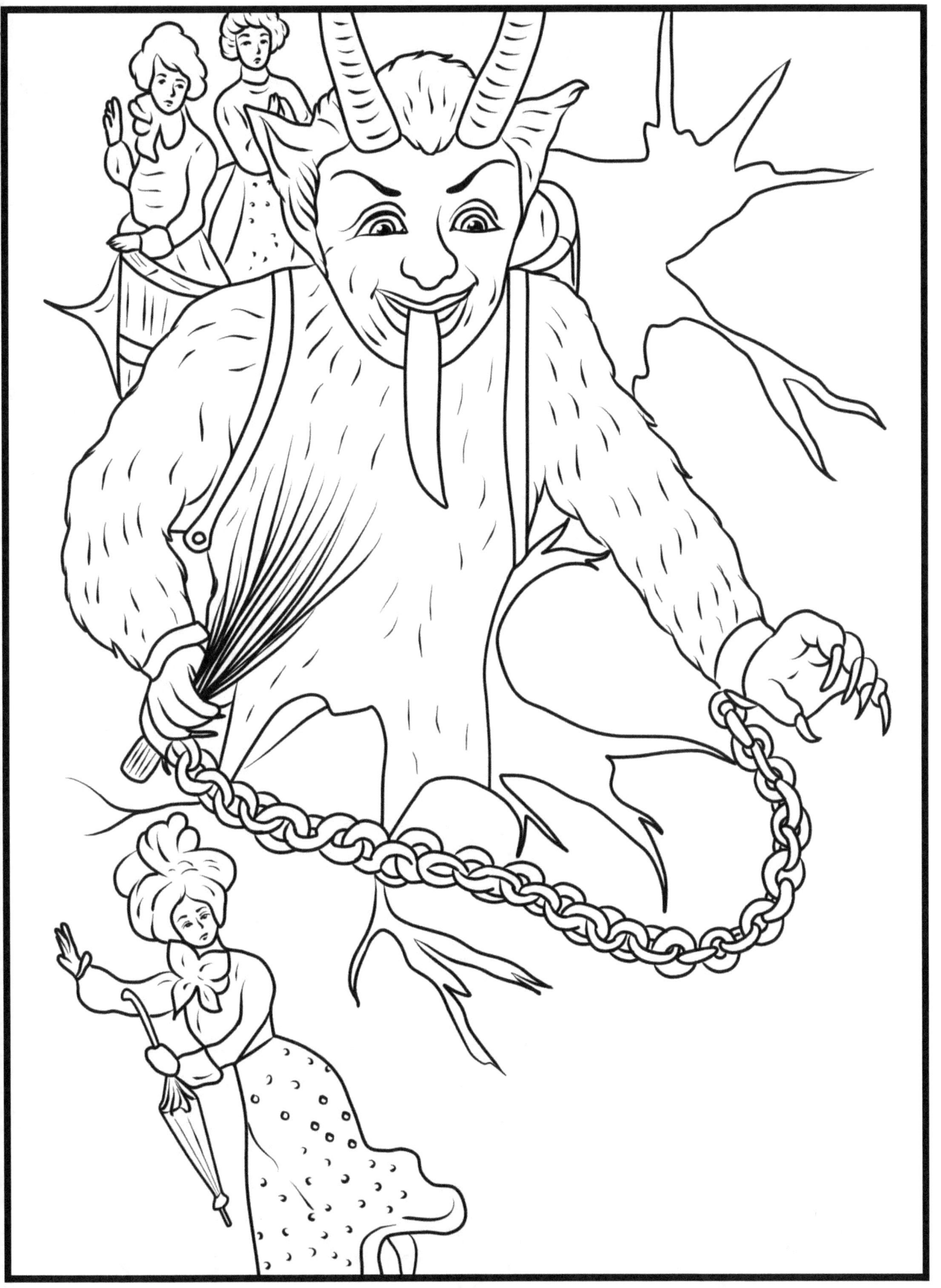

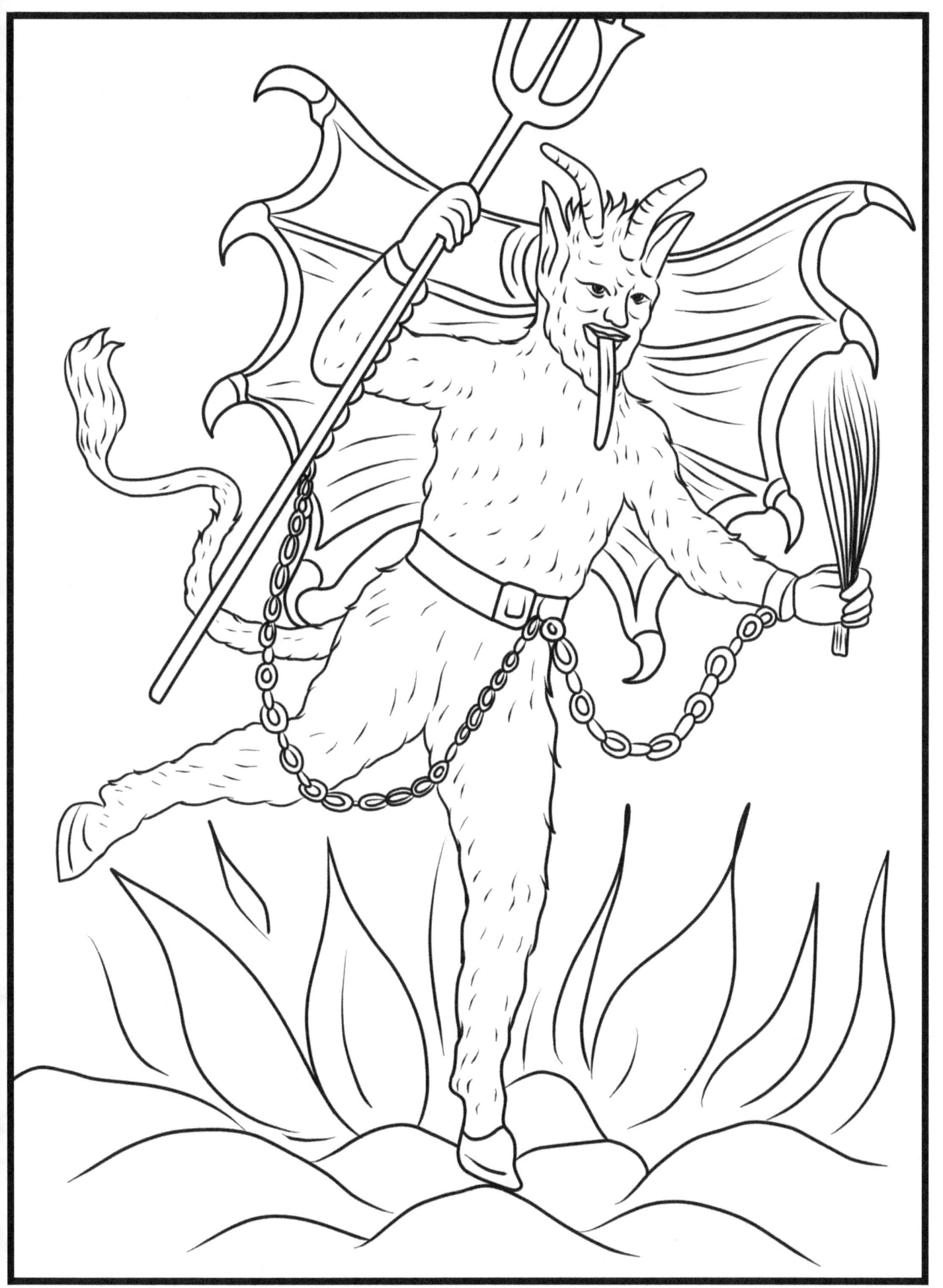

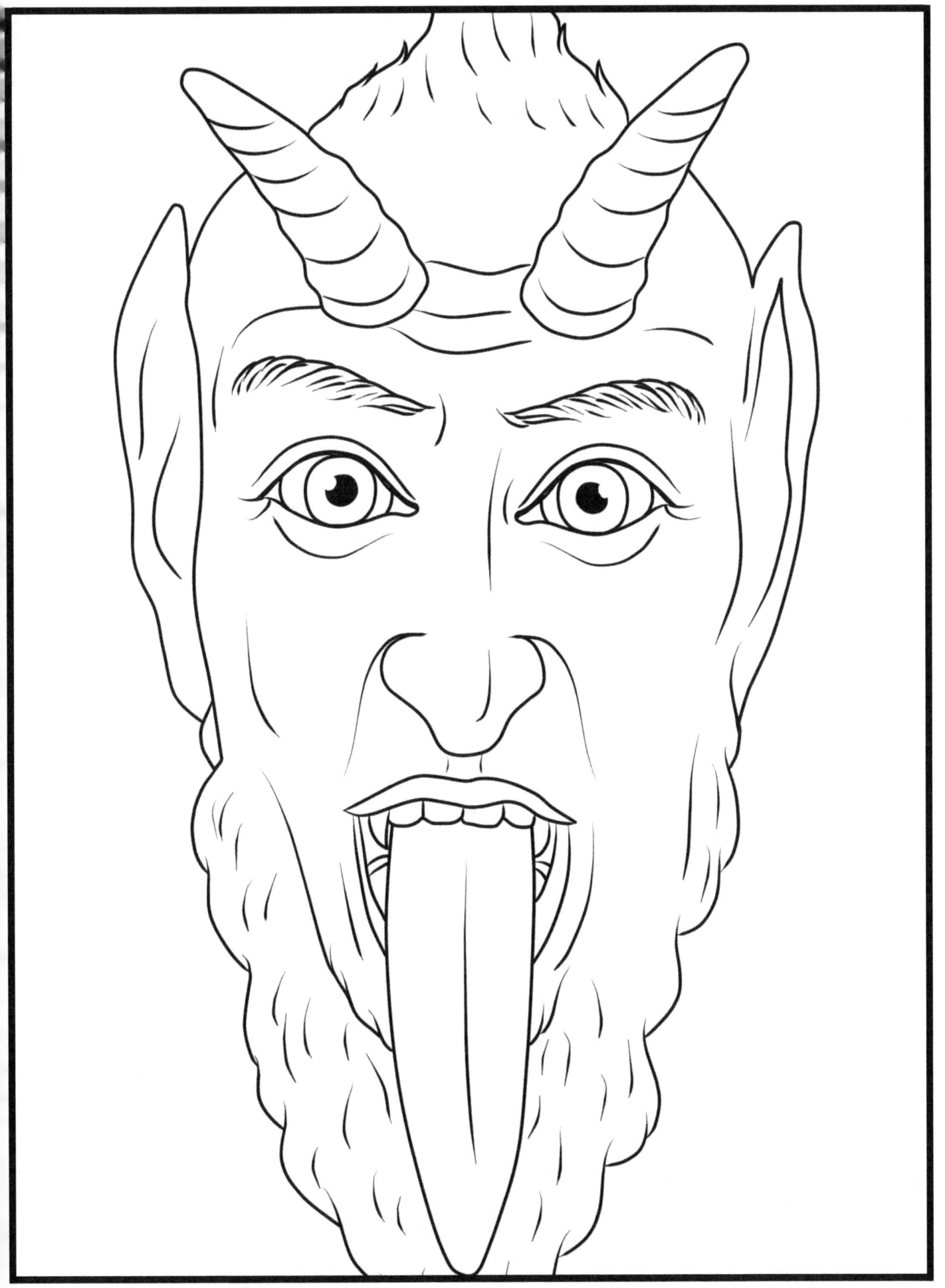

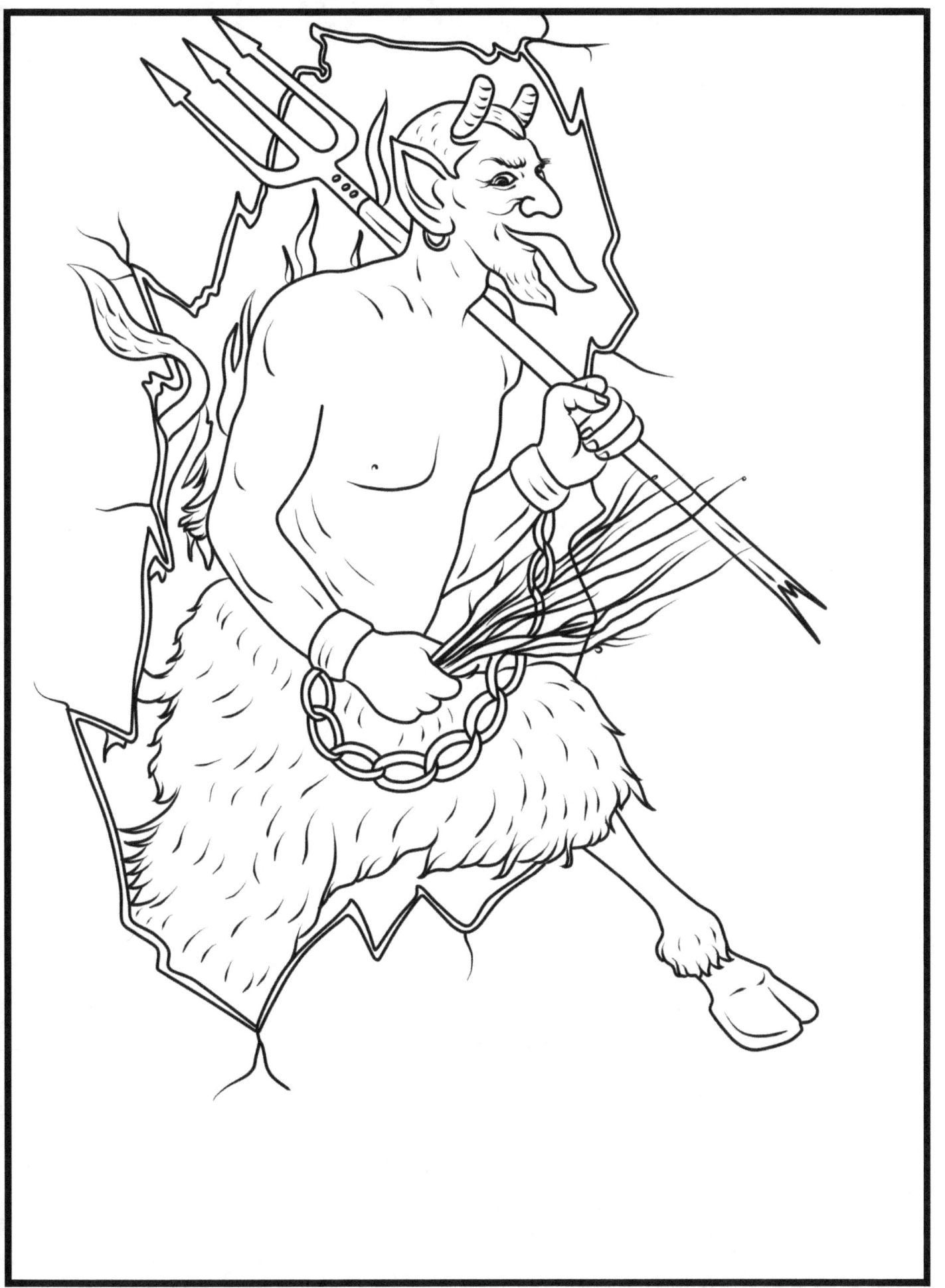

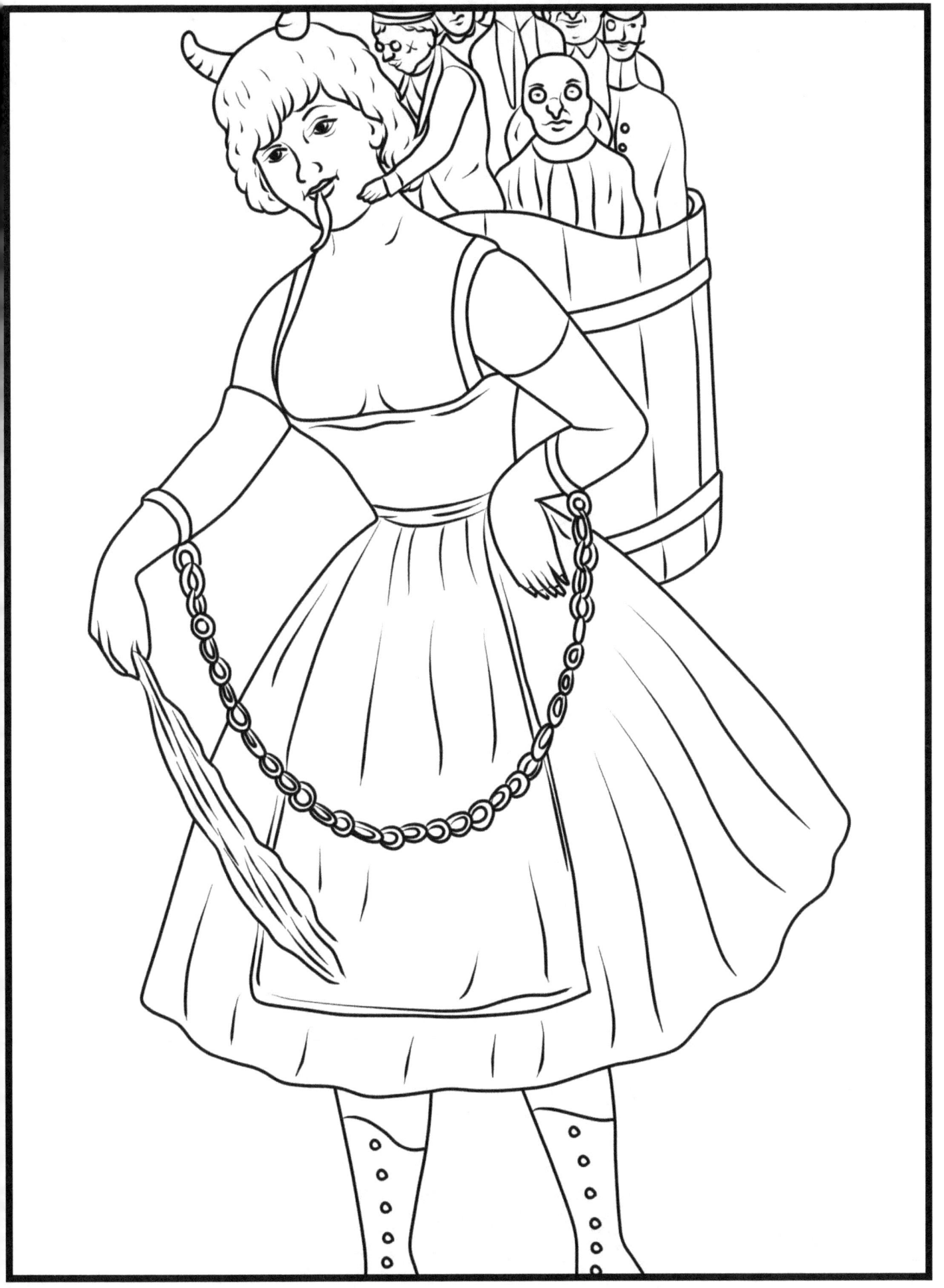

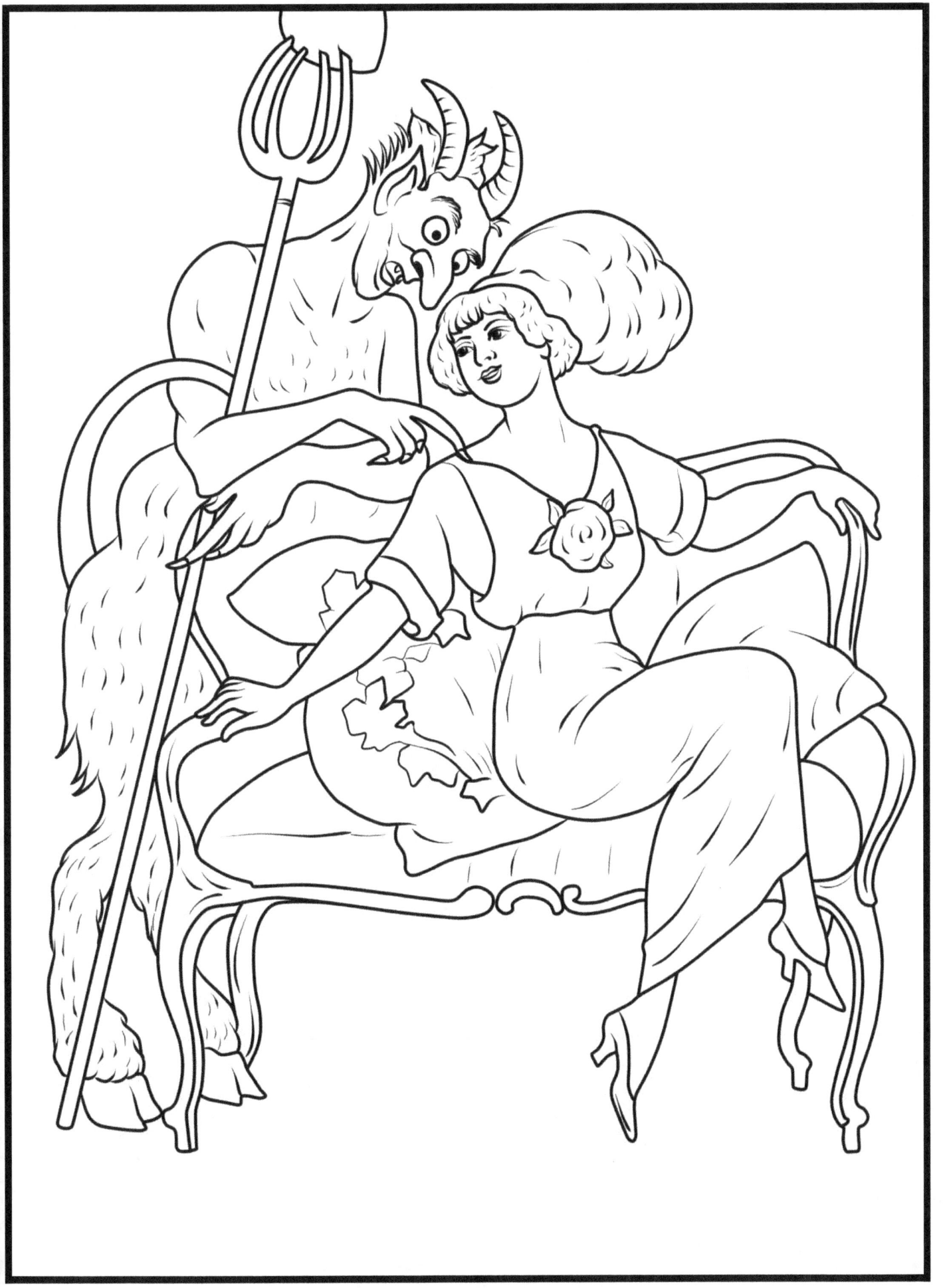

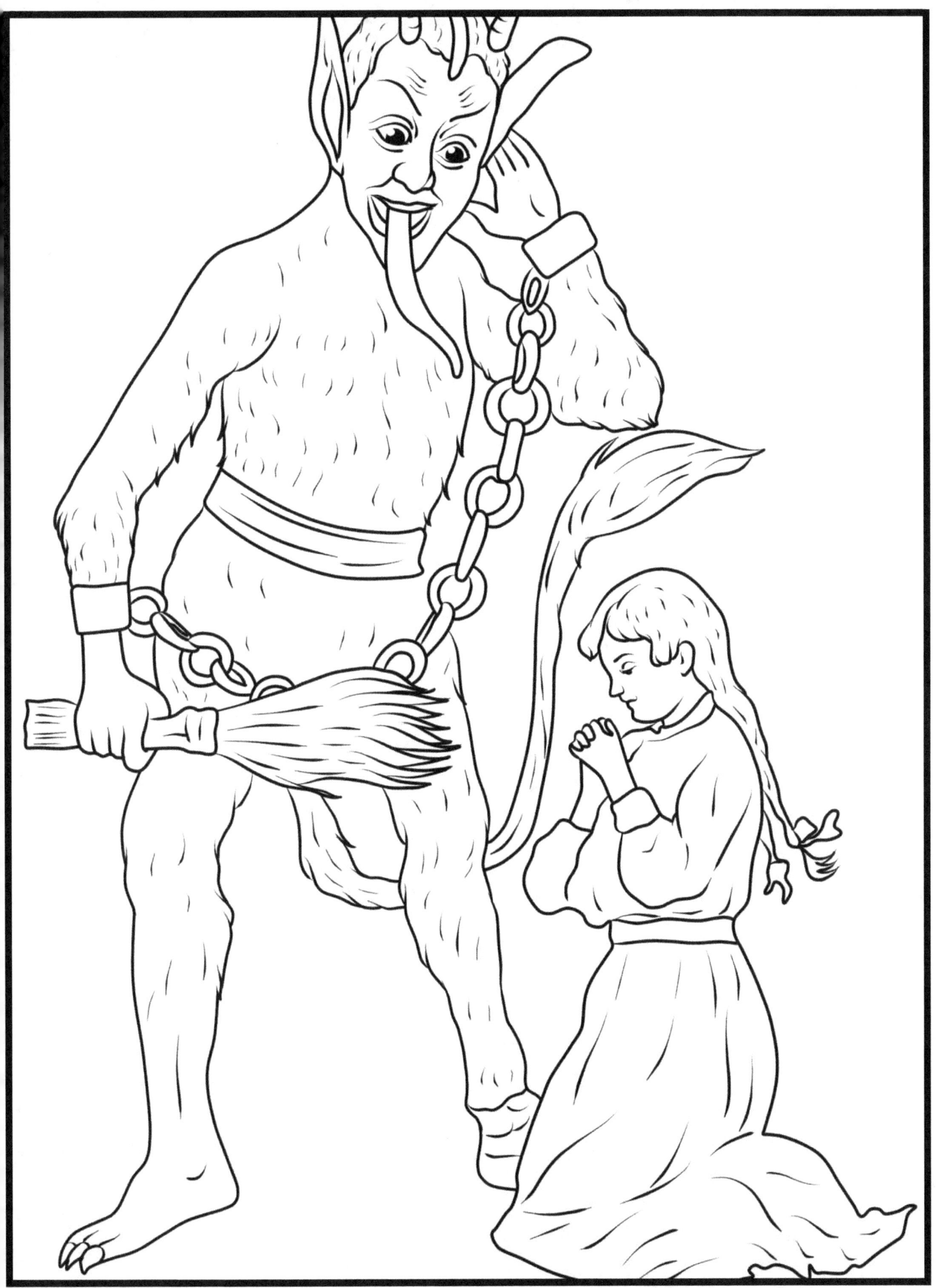

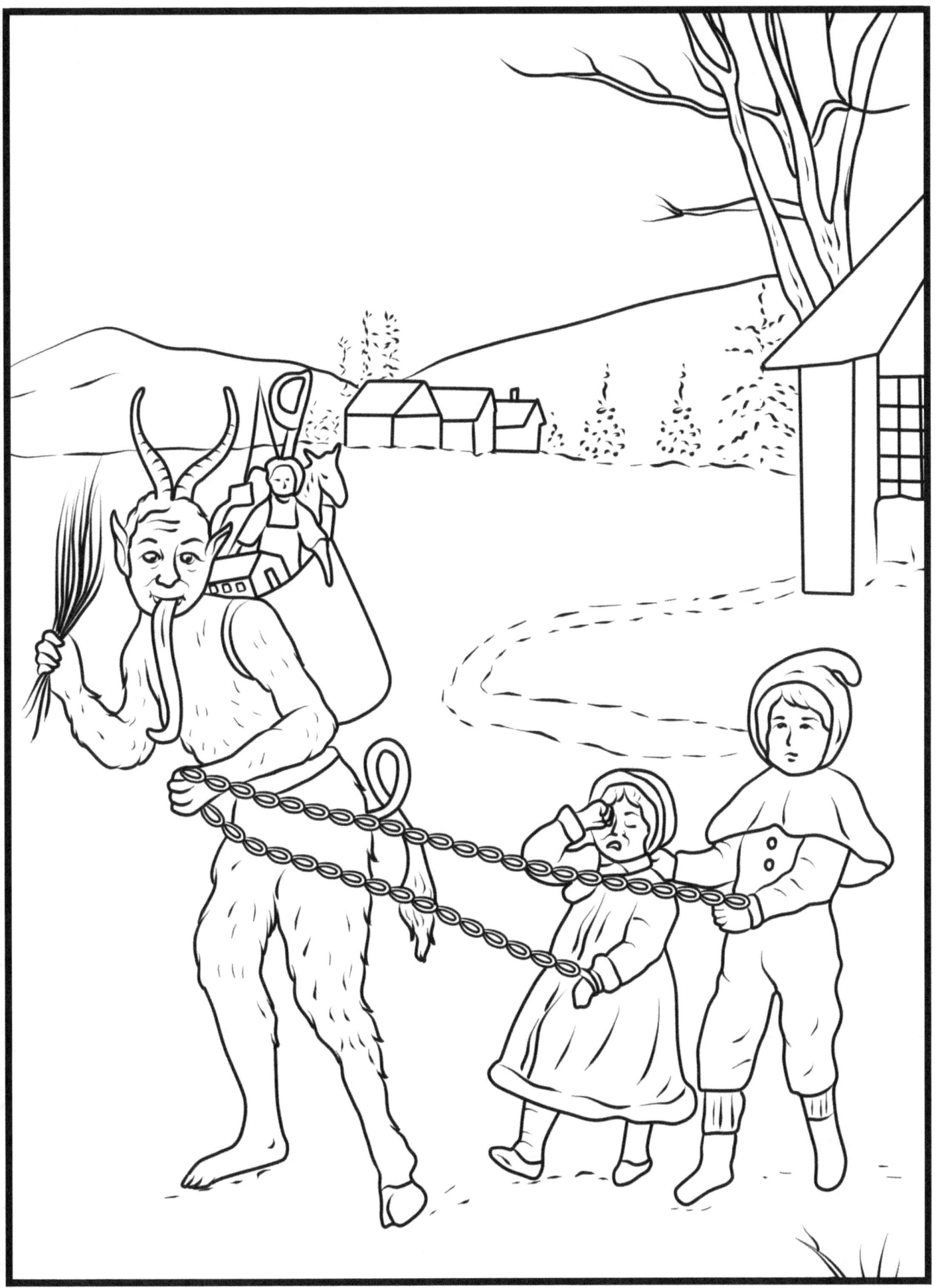

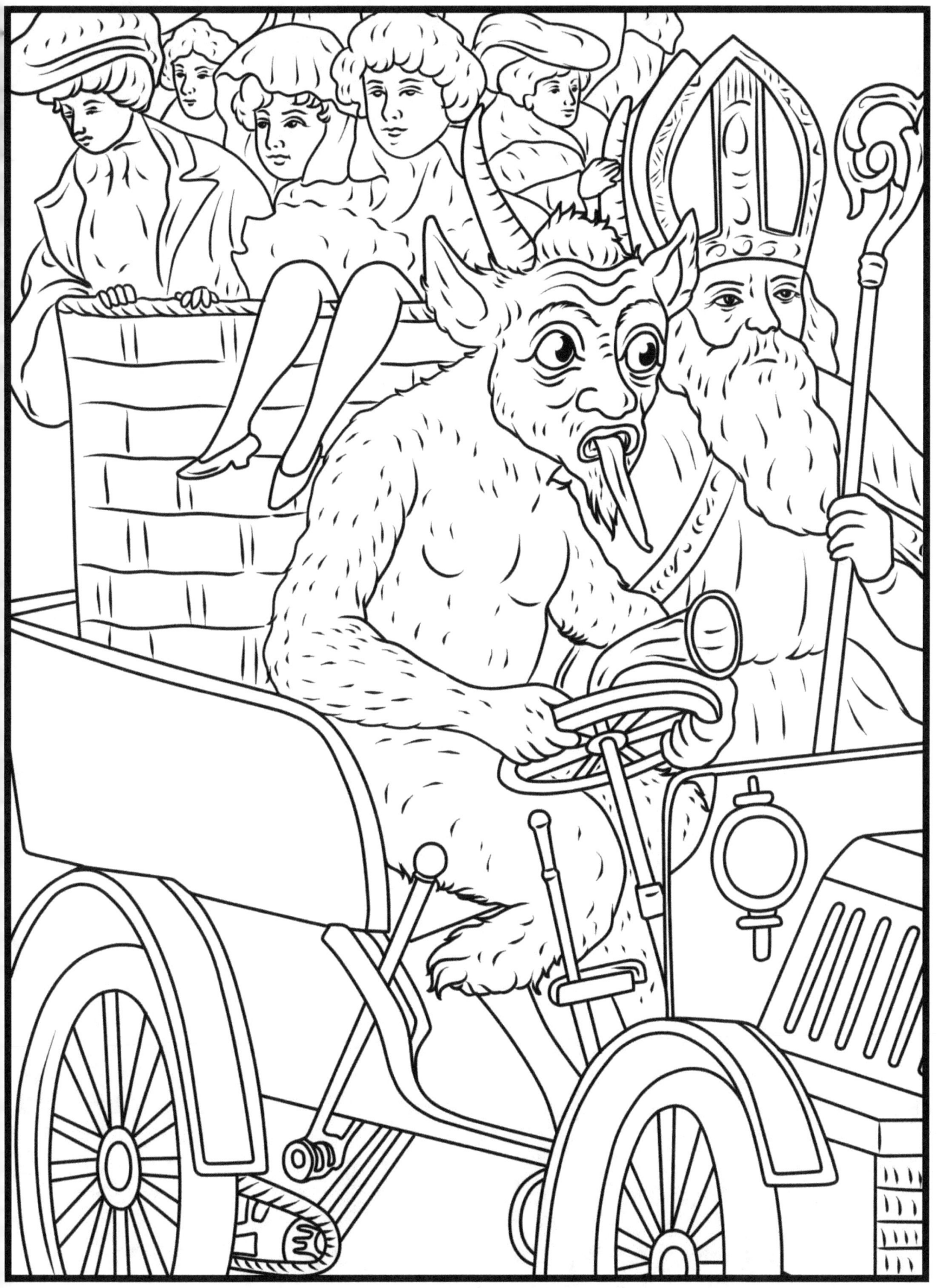

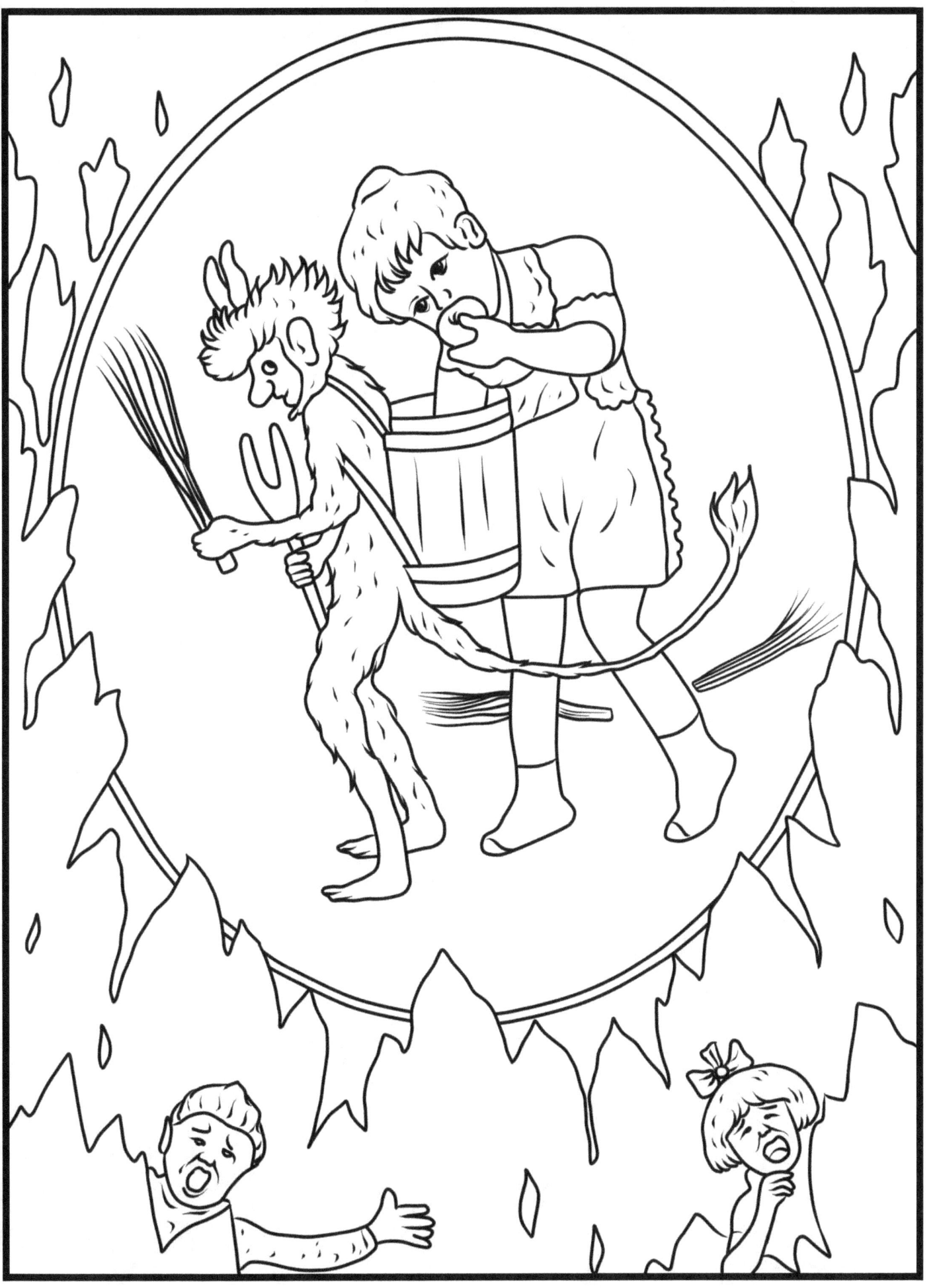

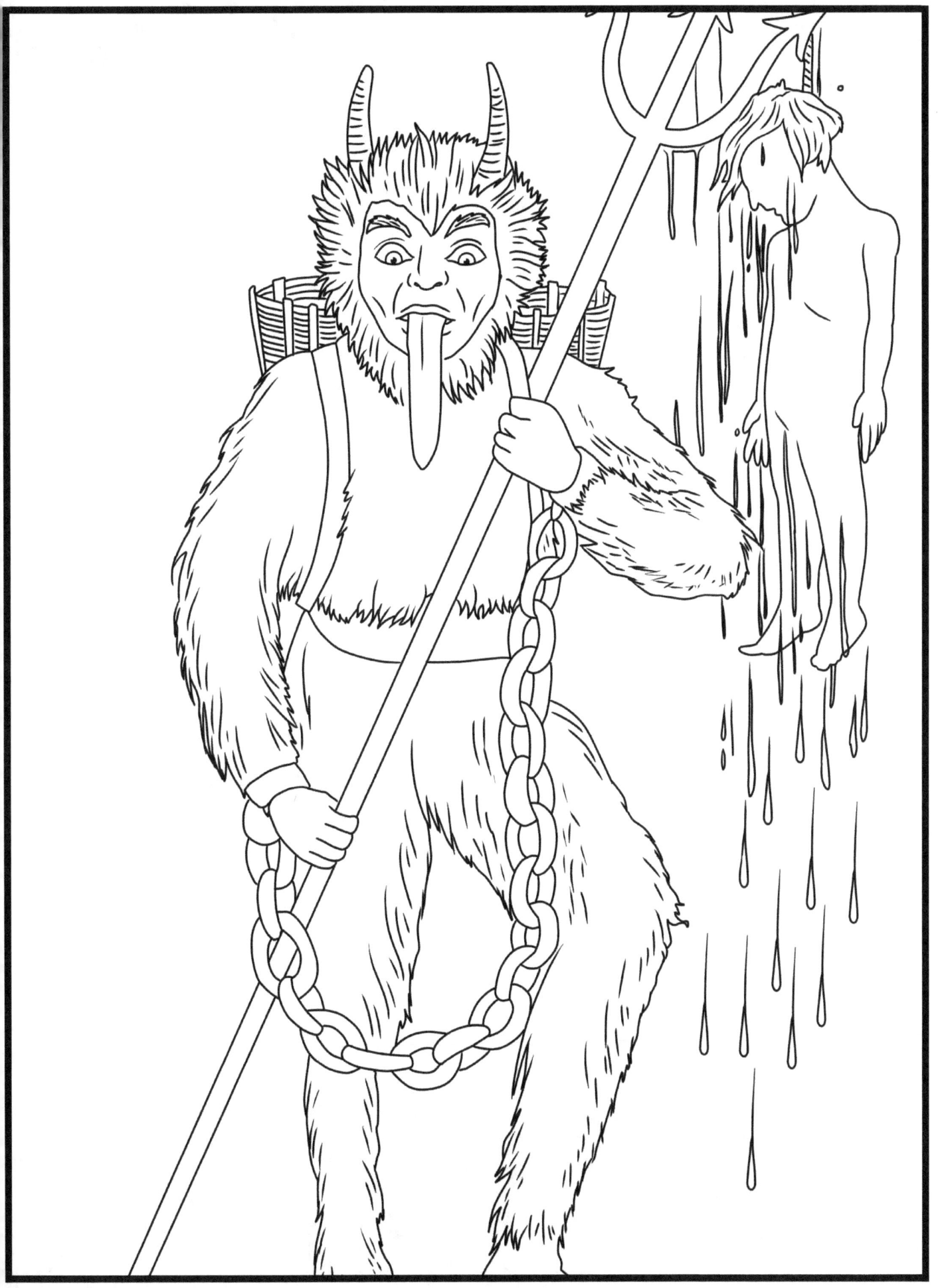

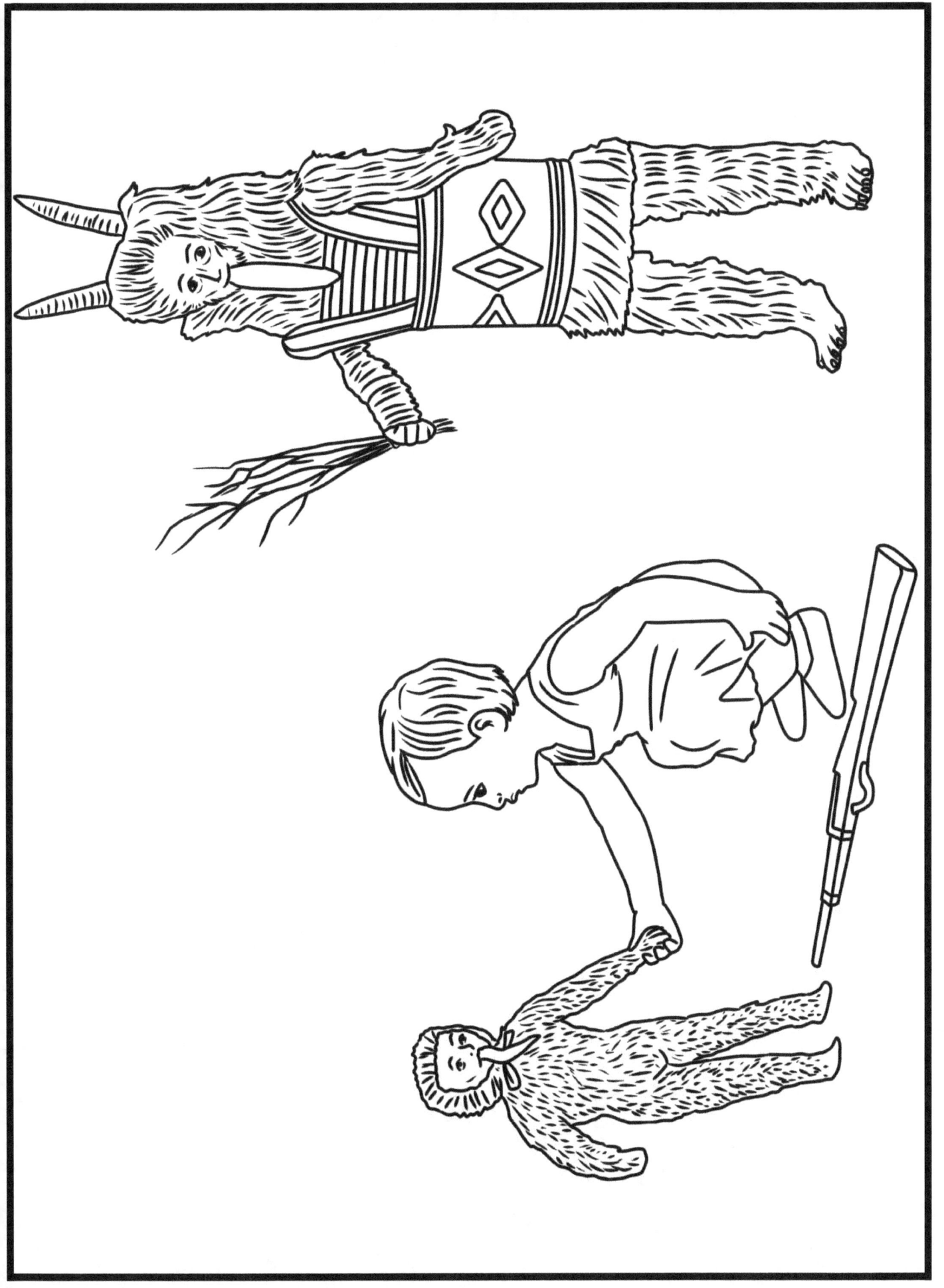

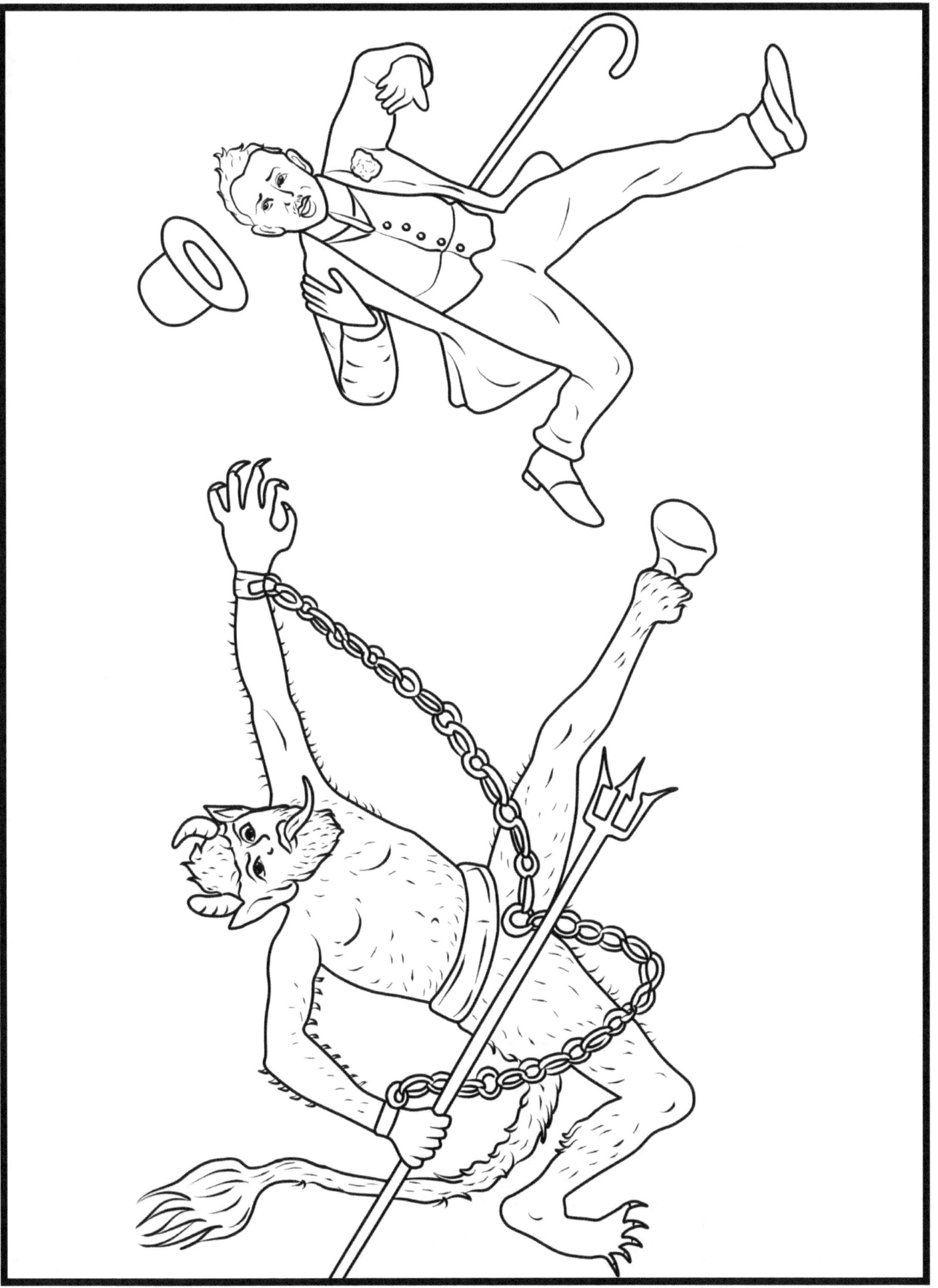

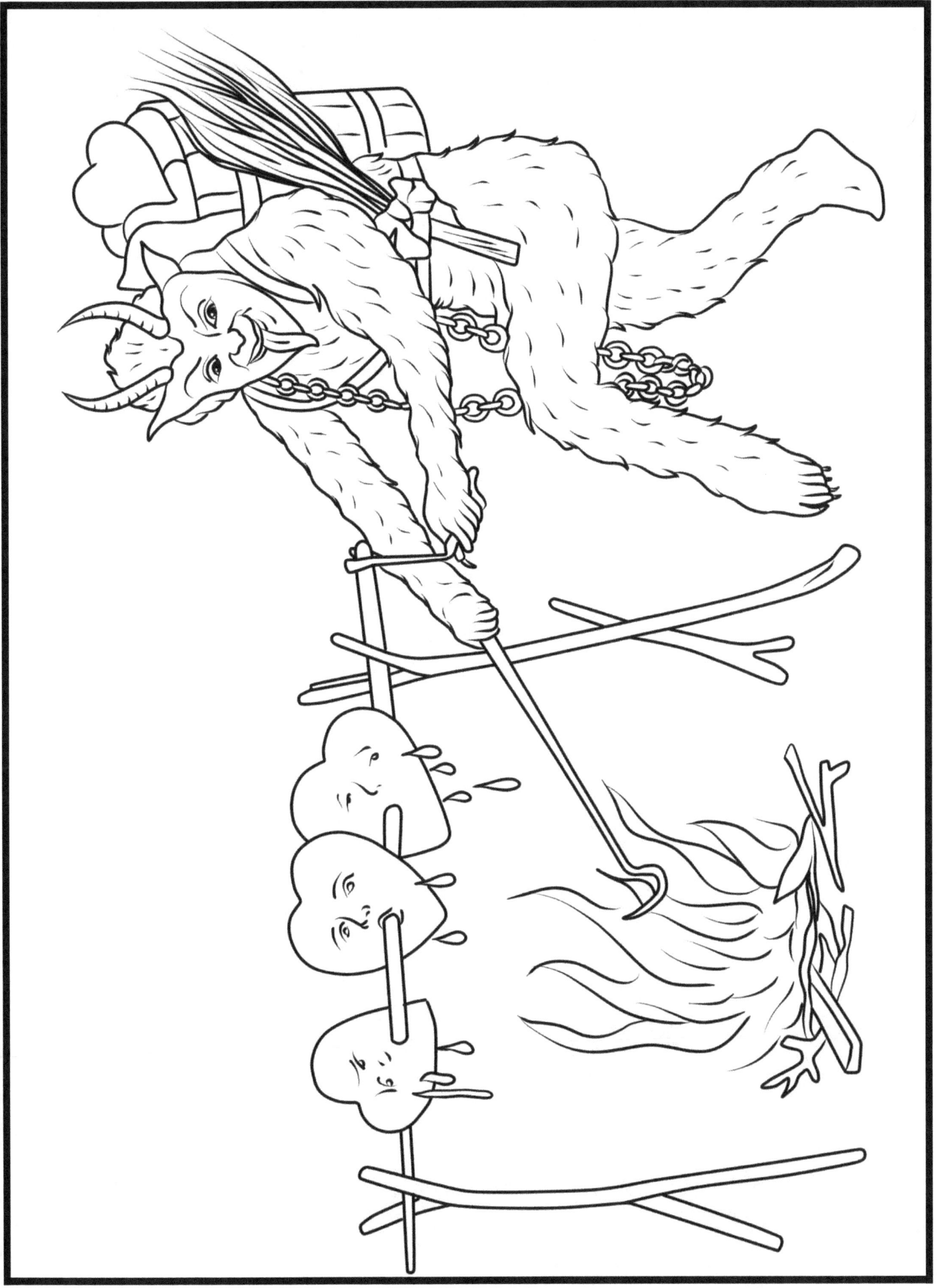

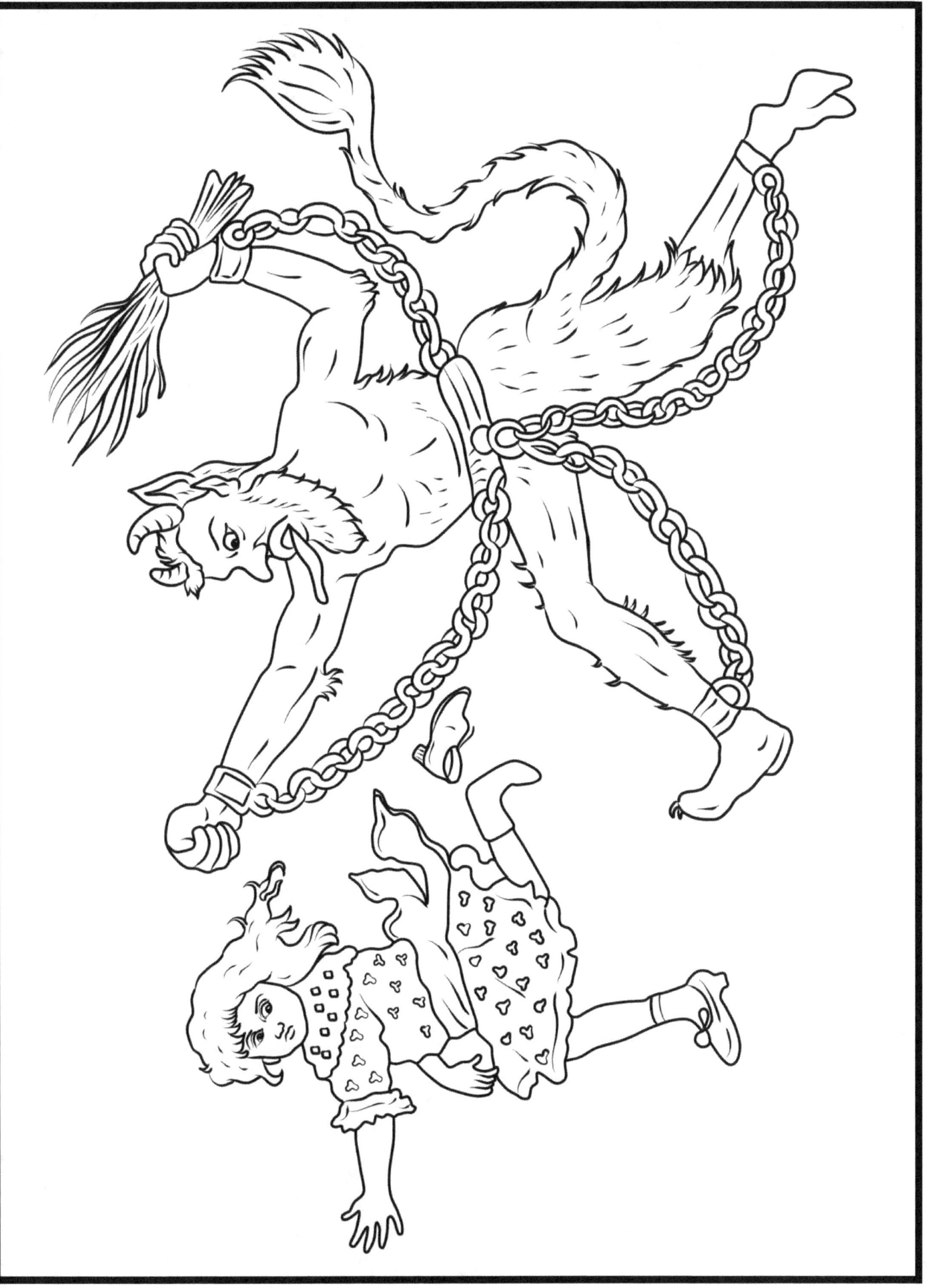

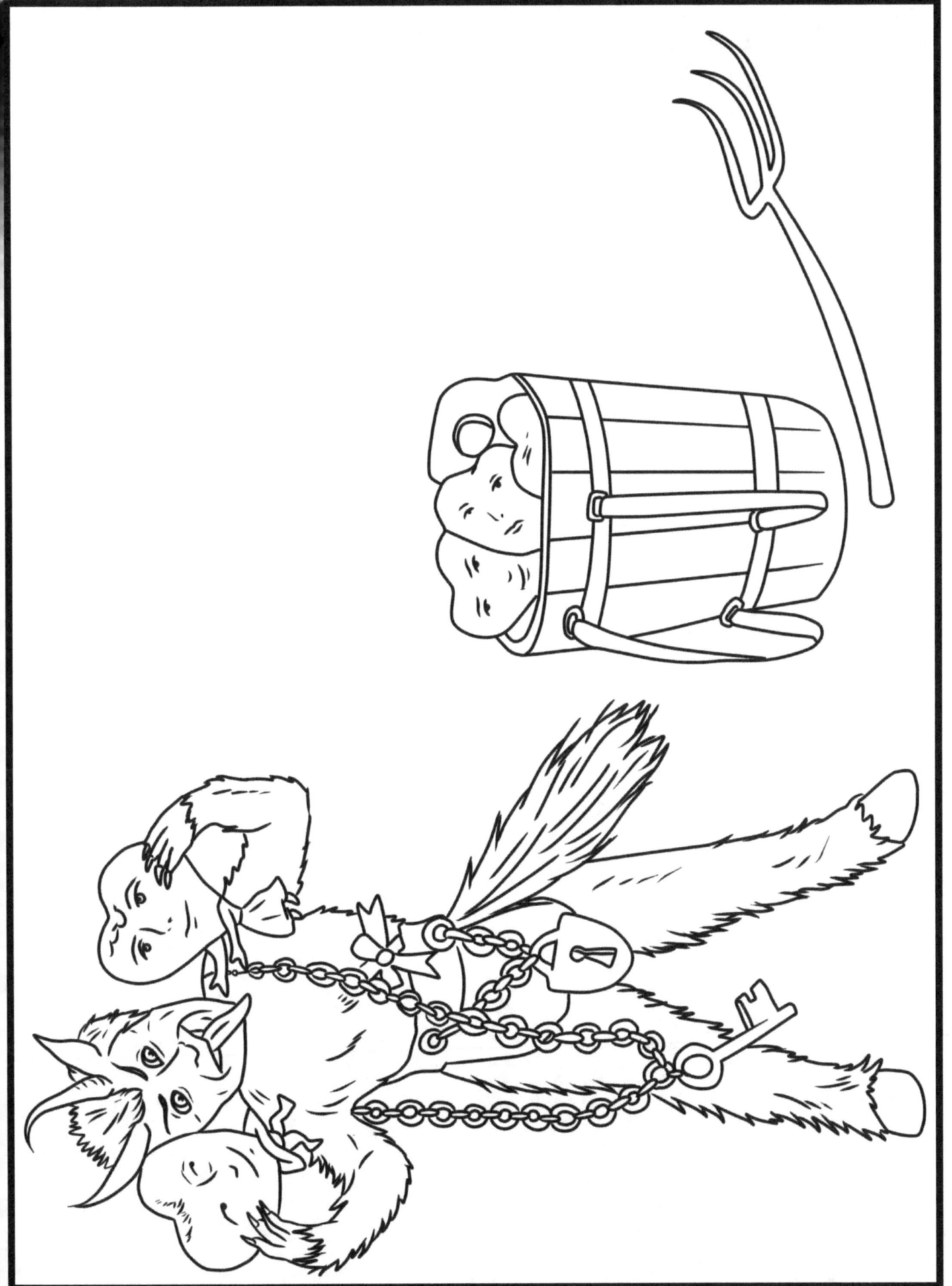

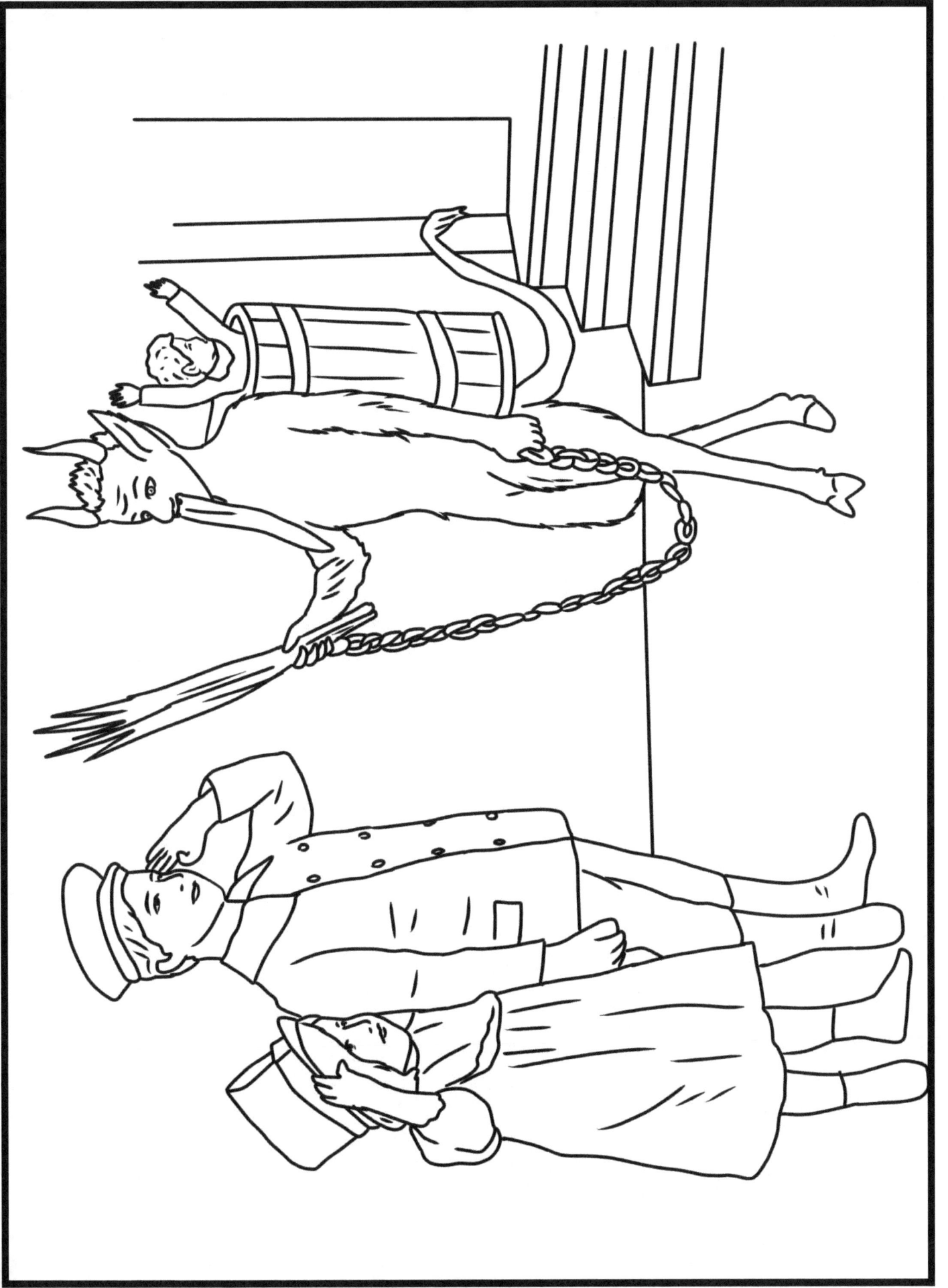

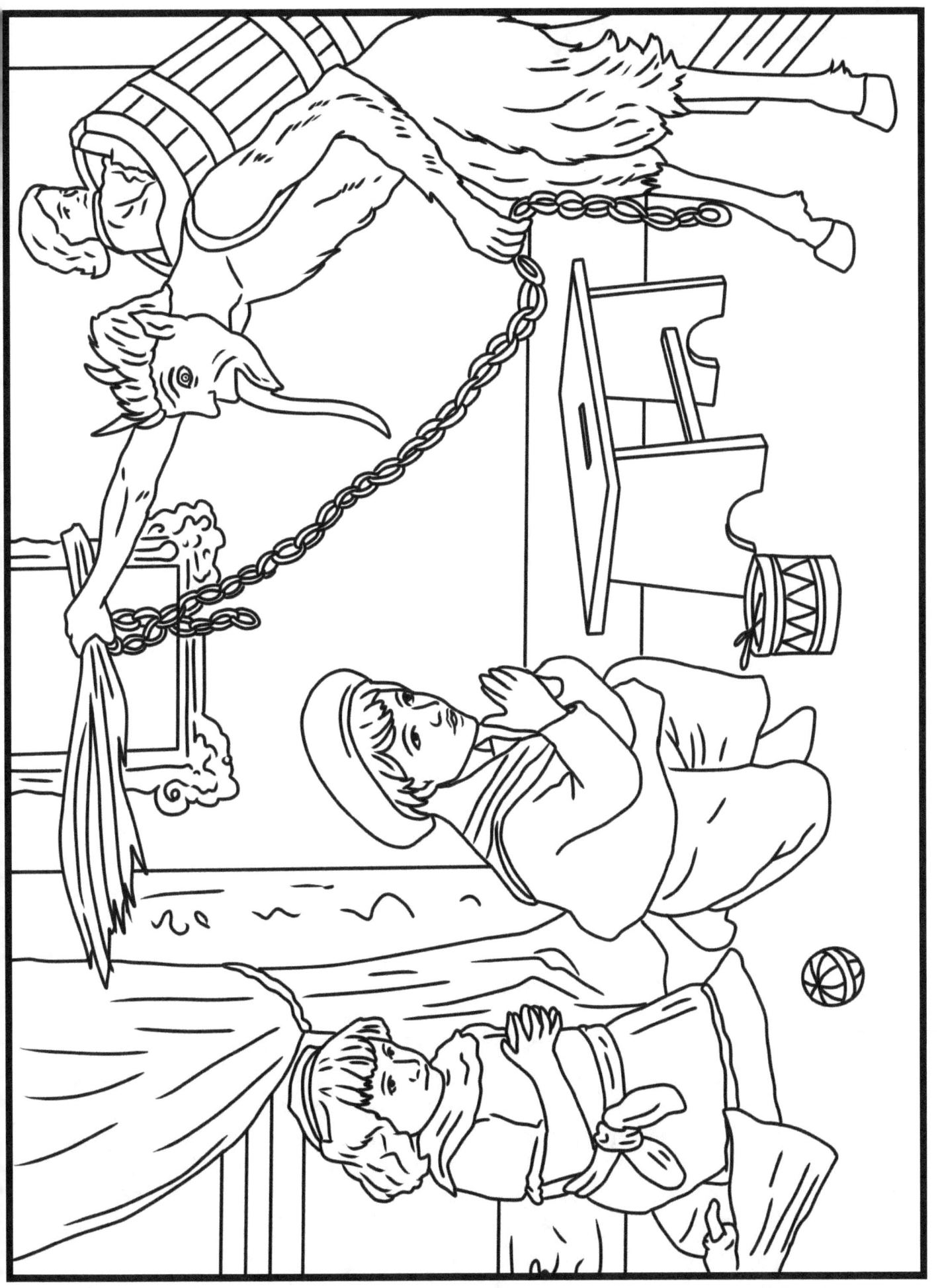

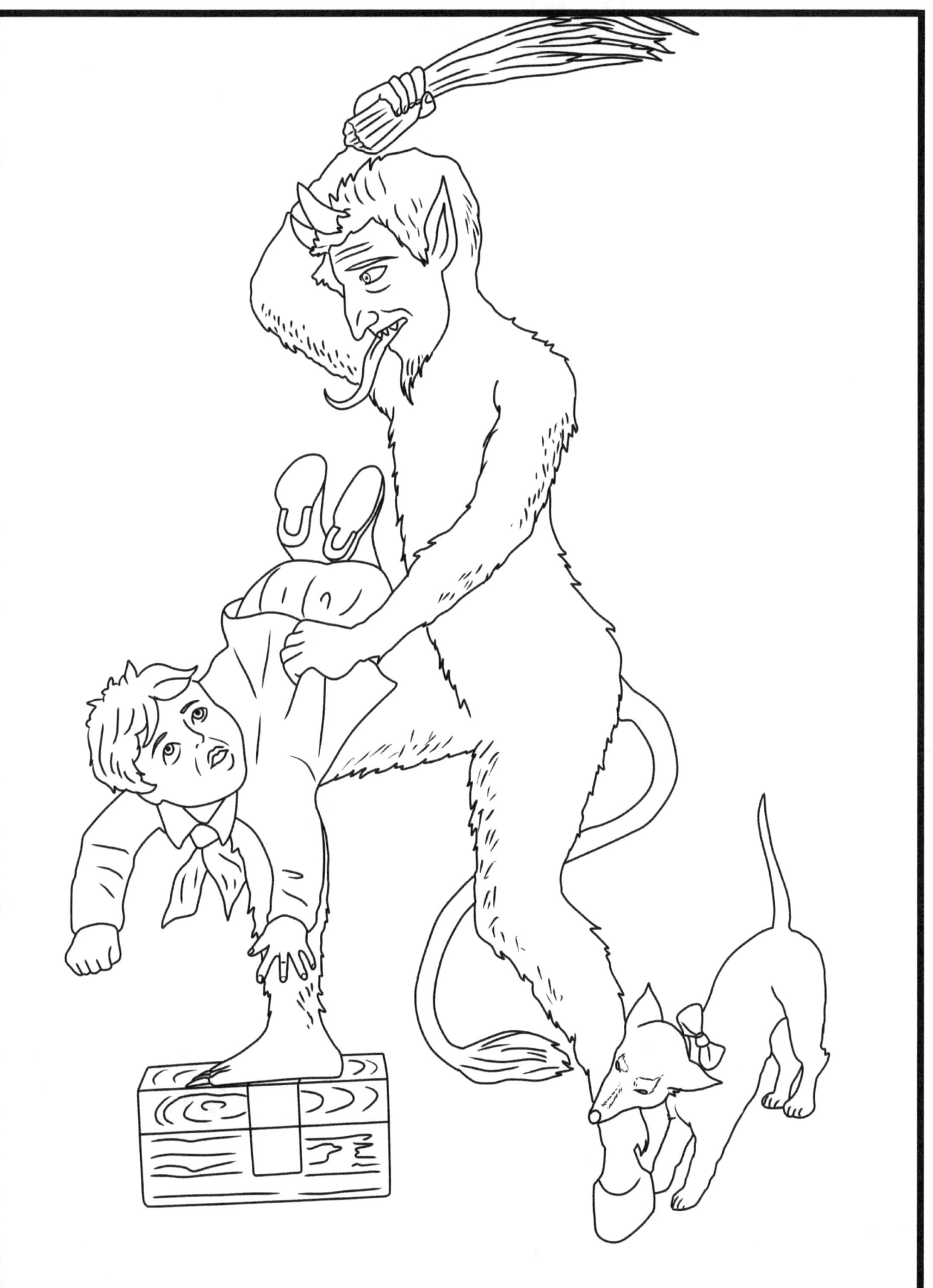

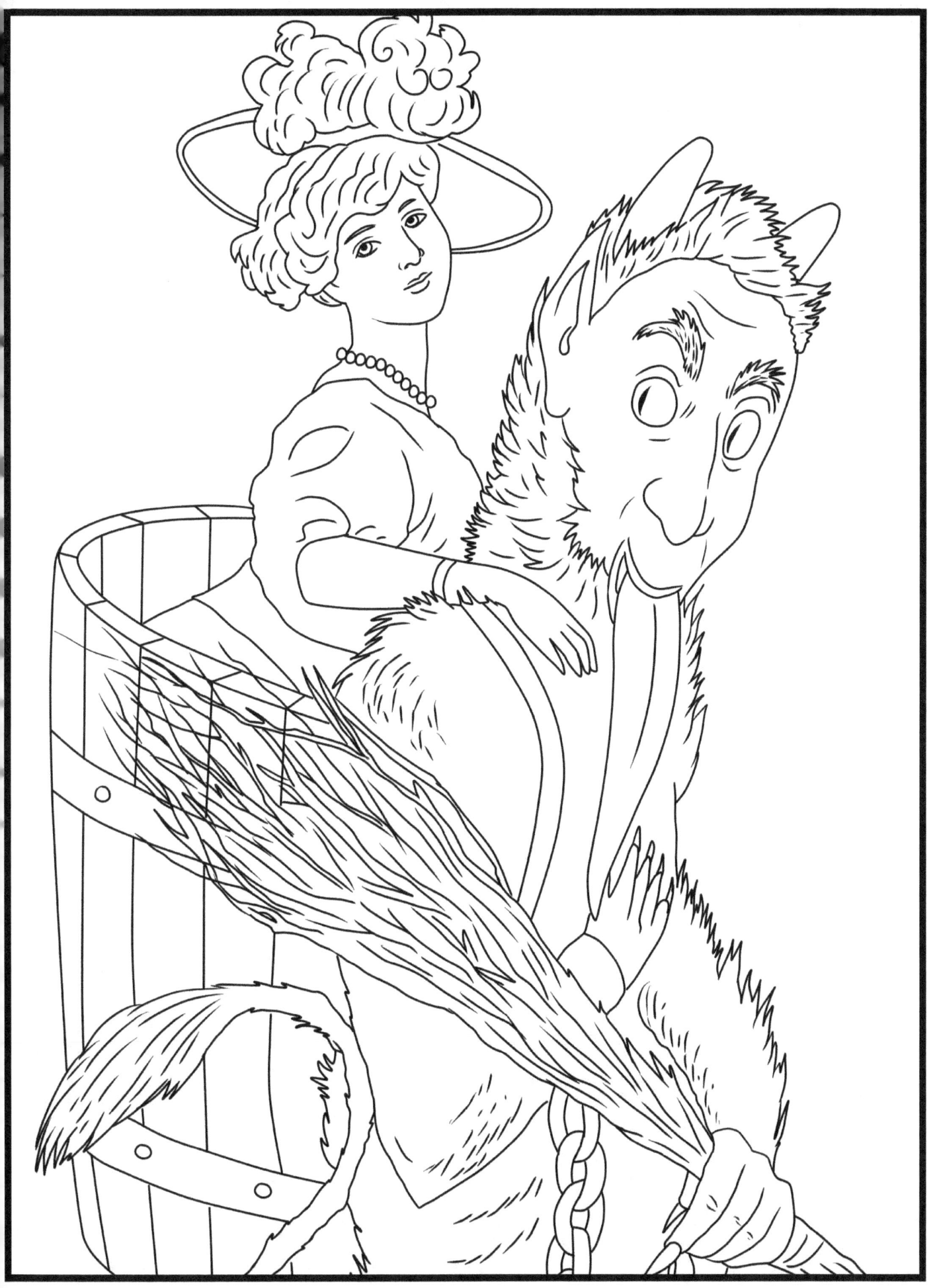

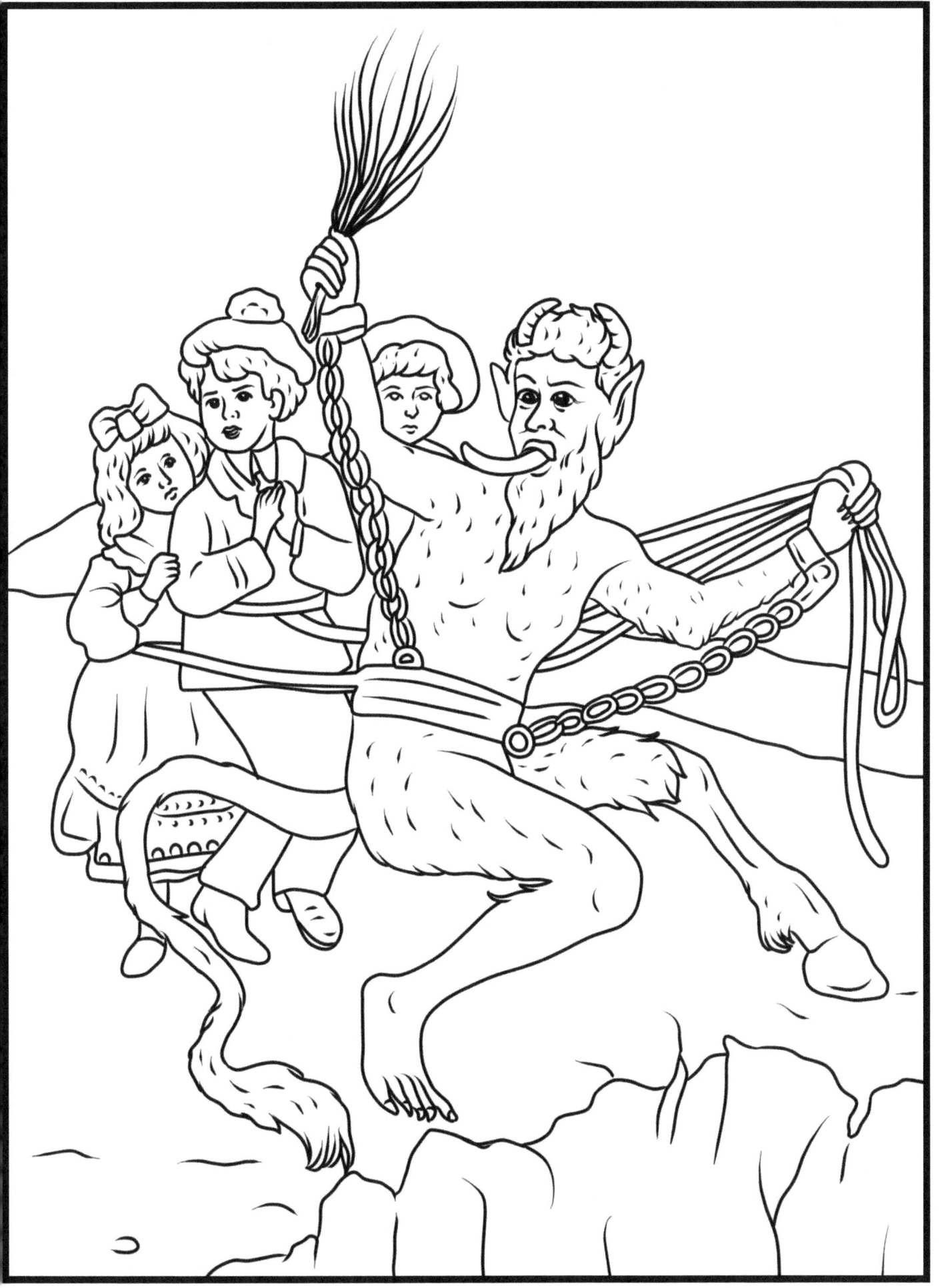

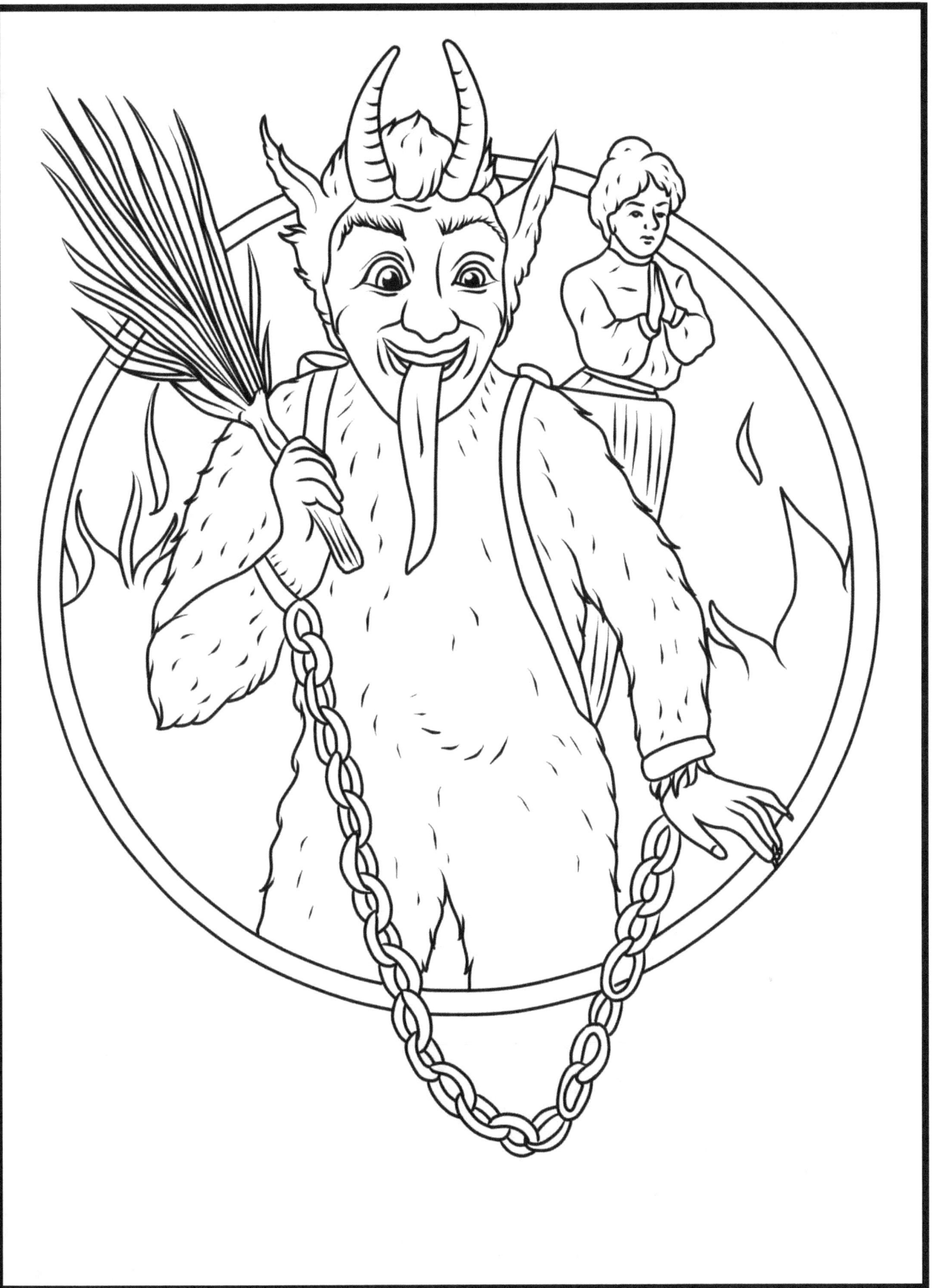

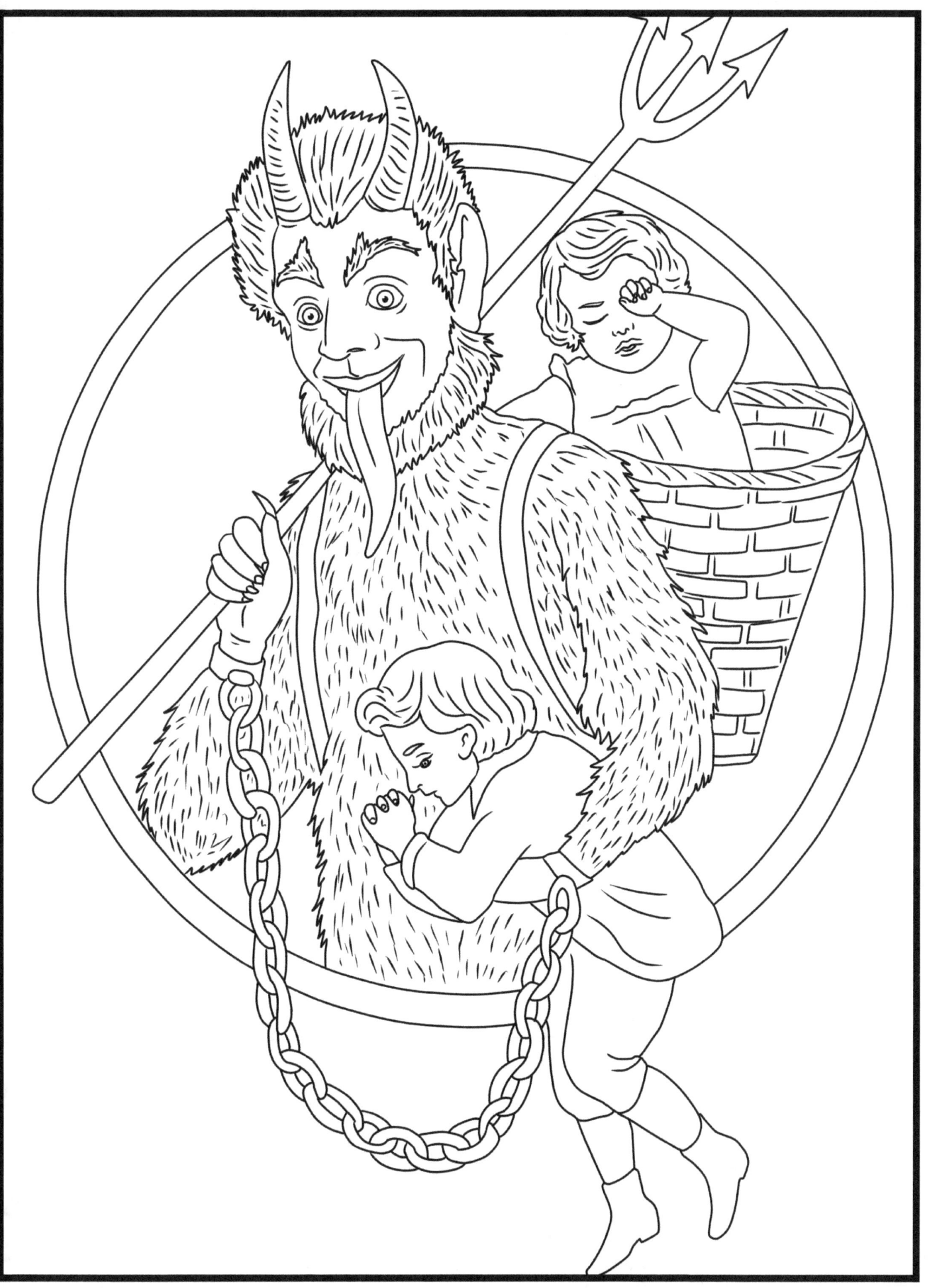

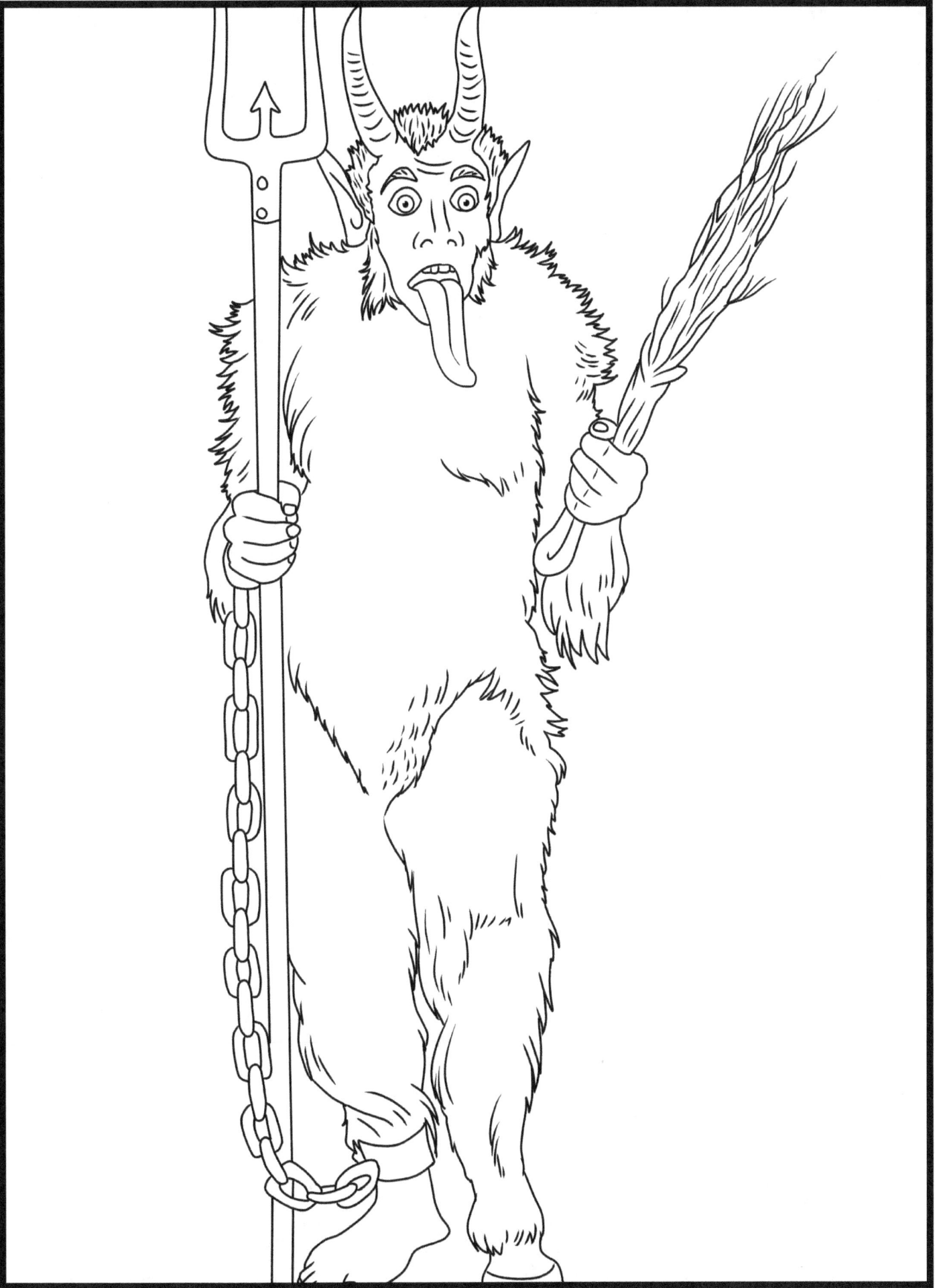

ABOUT THE AUTHOR

JORDAN COLTON IS AN AVID FAN OF HORROR. HE RESIDES IN UTAH WITH HIS CAT & HORROR FILM COLLECTION.

LEARN MORE ABOUT HIS COLORING BOOKS AT:
WWW.HORRIDCOLORINGBOOKS.COM

USE THE PROMO CODE "KRAMPUS" FOR FREE SHIPPING IN THE US.

CHECK OUT OUR OTHER COLORING BOOKS:
VOLUME 1: THE NIGHT OF THE LIVING DEAD
VOLUME 2: THE KRAMPUS VOL. 1
VOLUME 3: MANOS THE HANDS OF FATE
VOLUME 4: CREEPY CLOWNS
VOLUME 5 : DAHLIA'S DECREPIT DOLLS

www.ingramcontent.com/pod-product-compliance
Lightning Source LLC
Chambersburg PA
CBHW081119180526
45170CB00008B/2927